WHY AM I SHY?

Norman B. Rohrer
&
S. Philip Sutherland

AUGSBURG Publishing House • Minneapolis

WHY AM I SHY?

MANUFACTURED IN THE UNITED STATES OF AMERICA

*To the meek
who shall inherit the earth*

WHY AM I SHY?

*No one loves
him whom he fears.*

ARISTOTLE

FROM
THE
PUBLISHER

Everyone has experienced the distress of shyness. Most escape this self-made cultural prison through maturity; a surprising number do not.

Dr. Philip G. Zimbardo, professor of psychology at Stanford University in Palo Alto, California, surveyed 5000 high school and college students and found that 40% of the people questioned considered themselves to be shy. On a national scale that's approximately 85 million Americans. One in every 10 admitted to being "extremely shy."

This practical book identifies the types and causes of shyness and offers assistance in diminishing the disorder. *Why Am I Shy?* combines the work of two men. One is a layman who extricated himself from shyness to become one of the nation's most prolific Christian writers; the other is a psychotherapist who has a private practice in southern California and who serves also as a college professor of psychology.

A brief personal word from each author opens this presentation, the purpose of which is to help the timid unlock the doors of their mental cages and be free to enjoy life's fullest potential, for which God created them.

FROM
NORMAN
ROHRER

On the Pennsylvania truck farm where I grew up, my parents created a happy family atmosphere for their six active youngsters. Five developed socially; I became crippled by early shyness.

In grade school I had no close friends; parties were distressful; fulfilling relationships among peers were unknown. My unacceptable behavior haunted me. Had I been born passive? Or was shyness a black hole I had dug deliberately? The anxiety was so keen I quit the ninth grade in midyear. My father signed the papers for my release from the hated institution. At 14 my formal schooling was suspended and I retreated from people.

At 20 I drove a group of young men in our church to a southern university and stayed for a couple of days. My eyes had begun to develop astigmatism and were obviously being irritated without corrective glasses. One of my friends noticed the occasional watering and asked what was wrong. I tried to be funny by answering, "I want my mommie!"

Their derisive laughter and remarks made me boil. Too shy to flatten their noses and unable to explain my attempt at humor, I became determined to show them that I was not a mama's boy and that I could take care of myself. I returned home, packed a bag, and hit the road.

My perambulations took me through most of the States, Europe, the West Indies, Mexico, Alaska, and Canada. Eventually they led to Wheaton College in Illinois where I completed high school in two days through the General Educational Development tests, then enrolled in the college to earn a Bachelor of Arts degree four years later. Afterward I entered Grace Theological Seminary in Indiana and earned a Master of Divinity degree. In 1956 I summoned all my initiative and won the hand of a beautiful California girl. God has given us two sons.

The iron grip of shyness still tightens occasionally to let me know it's there, but it is now an enemy in submission. Looking back, I can see how God graciously opened doors to maturity and discharged me from the ranks of the timid.

Shy persons will understand their predicament better after encountering themselves on these pages. They will recognize the implications of perfectionism, manipulation, and misdirected anger which the shy endure. But if the escape route is followed carefully, they will not be the same persons next year as they are now.

It is my prayer that God will liberate all who read this book as he liberated me.

The new way is better than the old.

FROM
PHILIP
SUTHERLAND

My colleague's struggles with shyness have been encountered by more people than is generally imagined. Everybody, to a greater or lesser degree, suffers from shyness, but few understand its nature and function.

My office is visited by scores of shy people every week. You'll meet some of them as they appear with assumed names in this book. These clients are finding exciting new ways to release the grip of this crippling emotion. Shyness diminishes as new feelings and reactions emerge and as clients develop more active modes of handling situations and people.

Dramatic, instant change happens only on television and in cheap novels; it is rare among the psychotherapist's congress of clients. Most often deliverance is slow, but growth out of shyness, though gradual, is available for *all persons of all ages.*

I have seen preschool children change from timid, withdrawn little pitiables into active, involved persons. Clients in their 40s and 50s have altered their behavior and expansively drawn new social guidelines. Some even in their 60s and 70s have blossomed into new people.

Shy persons are not victims of their plight, and no shy person is doomed to a lifetime of suffering. This book explains why you are shy, shows how to understand your ongoing fears, and suggests ways to change your thinking and find deliverance.

To determine your present degree of shyness, take the self-analysis that follows. It is not a test. There are no correct or incorrect answers. It is designed to give you insight into your suffering and its causes. When you have completed it, lay it aside and begin to read the book. It is important that you complete this self-analysis *before* you read the book.

It is not possible to become perfectly bold and socially fearless. Such a goal is unrealistic. But if, armed with knowledge, you are willing to face the Dragon Shyness and slay it, you have pulled the latchstring on your prison door.

SELF-ANALYSIS

*(Complete before
reading this book)*

This analysis is designed to give you personal insights. When you have finished, turn to page 126 and interpret your responses.

1. Draw a circle, a square, a star, and the figure S. Using any or all of these symbols, doodle for 15 minutes on a separate piece of paper.

2. Pretend you're in a play with the following cast:

Hero	Daughter	Nurse
Heroine	Father	Teacher
Villain	Mother	Bank president
Butler	Oldest child	Maid
Son	Youngest child	Mayor

Which role would you want to play and why? Which role would your friends select you for and why?

3. If you had to become an animal, which one would you want to be and why?

4. Of all famous people, real or fictional, past or present, who would you like to be and why?

5. Prepare an essay on your feelings regarding your sexuality. Express freely your fantasies and fears. Include all your thoughts regarding persons of the opposite sex and your own behavior toward them. Honesty is essential.

6. Write separately a shyness autobiography. Begin with your earliest memories and record briefly the times when shyness was a painful experience for you. Bring it up to the immediate present. Include situations, feelings, fears, and fantasies.

7. Complete the following sentences:

a. Most people need _____

_____

b. I am happiest when _____

_____

c. When I was a child _____

_____

d. The thing I like best about me _____

_____

e. The worst thing about me is _____

_____

f. My mother _____

_____

g. My father _____

_____

h. Boys _____

_____

i. Girls _____

_____

j. I get embarrassed when _____

_____

k. I feel strongest when _____

_____

l. When in doubt, I _____

_____

m. I wish _____

_____

n. I hate _____

_____

o. People shouldn't _____

_____

p. If I were a ruler, I _____

_____

q. Nobody ever _____

_____

1 | WHY YOU ARE SHY

The brave and bold persist even against fortune; the timid and cowardly rush to despair through fear alone.

TACITUS

Work at the factory had been extra tiring that day, but the mill hand was now home in his easy chair reading the evening paper.

Suddenly he folded the last section and laid it aside. He smiled mischievously as he selected a favorite hi-fi recording and touched the needle to the wax. As great swells of spirited music filled the humble dwelling, his wife dried her hands at the kitchen sink, hurried into the living room, and caught his hands. The couple whirled about the room. Now they hugged, now they twirled each other playfully as the cadence of the harmonious beat rose and fell.

"Would you love me more if I were the President?" he whispered, kissing her ear.

"No," his wife replied, her apron swinging wide in an extra whirl.

"Why not?" he queried.

"Because," she answered coyly, a blush on her plain cheek, "I'd be much too shy."

Most of us would probably experience a moment of shyness before the President, and we smile at the woman's beguiling honesty. But for millions of Americans, shyness is nothing to smile about. They are paralyzed by timidity even among relatives, neighbors, and friends. The scourge of shyness destroys careers, shatters dreams, puts a strain on marriages, and keeps its victims shackled to hated patterns of behavior in which they can't love themselves, others, or God as they would like.

Shy people, to a greater or lesser degree, believe themselves to be victims of earlier situations. "I'm shy," they contend, "because I was born that way," or "because my mother never gave me any encouragement," or "because an older brother could do everything right and I couldn't keep up," or "because I had a beautiful sister and I always felt inferior," or "because my strong-willed father intimidated me."

People who believe they have been forced into shyness by their environment see little hope of redirecting their lives. Movies, books, and television entertainment strengthen these convictions, presenting people as victims of their background, as if they had no choice in the way they developed.

Such views are overly simple and inaccurate. They

keep persons convinced they are crippled permanently by shyness. When shy people get a more complete and accurate view of themselves and the causes of their problem, they begin to have hope, confidence, and—most important—a change of feeling and behavior.

Change begins with the recognition of this radical but accurate perspective of human behavior: *People are not merely victims of their environment.*

How other people treat us is, of course, important. But the essence of personality development is not how we are treated but how we choose to respond to the way we are treated.

Take as an example two children. Each spills paint on the floor while doing art activities at school. One child simply gets some towels and cleans it up without panic or fear; the other runs and hides in the bathroom because of embarrassment. Each child chooses to behave in the way that seems most efficient at the moment. Their environment is identical, but their responses are quite dissimilar.

Two sisters get into trouble and their parents scream and condemn. When the girls are told to go to their rooms, the older daughter chooses to cry and feel naughty while the younger daughter goes promptly to her room, entertains herself, and concludes that she has done nothing wrong, despite the trouble she caused others.

Each of these children responded in a different way in the same environment. Each choice was made with the motive of protecting the individual from psychological insult. The older girl, to keep the love of her parents, gladly acknowledged her guilt; the younger girl had to maintain her "perfection." Any admission of error would make her feel completely worthless. So she maintained her perfect self-image by denying error.

Two men, fired from identical jobs, respond quite differently. The first man accepts it as one of those disappointments that is part of living and begins immediately to seek other employment. The other fellow feels insulted, hurt, unloved. He chooses to go to a bar and diminish his feelings through drinking.

Again, the same circumstances but different responses to the circumstances. Each choice is dependent on the personality of the chooser. How a person acts and reacts depends on hundreds of choices made throughout that individual's history. Most choices are so automatic that they appear to be not choices but merely something that we couldn't help but do. Much of our behavior *seems* to be involuntary because we have made similar choices in hundreds of different circumstances. But every time we respond to our environment, we are actively choosing.

A beautiful 30-year-old divorced woman who grew up in a rural community made wrong choices early in her life and suffered because of them.

When Myrna was small she often sat on the couch with her father, whom she almost worshiped.

The youngster was so pleased by her father's show of love and attention that she sat perfectly still without saying or doing anything. She reasoned: If I say anything, the spell might be broken and Daddy might go away. So she chose to do and say nothing because to her that seemed the only way to avoid the risk of losing her father's attention.

Myrna has chosen to do and say nothing so often and in so many circumstances that passivity has become automatic. Result: extreme shyness. But she *did choose* her behavior. She remembers thinking of things she might say to her father, but she always censored them to maintain her daddy's attention.

Other children, under the same circumstances, would choose a more active way to keep their father's attention. They might talk to him or hug him or ask questions or beg him to read to them. Children choose on the basis of what they feel will be most satisfying at the moment.

Shyness is not something a person *has,* nor is it totally accurate to say a person *is* shy. The term "shy" is applied to persons who in many situations choose to act in a shy manner because they feel it is psychologically safe.

Passivity—a choice, not a chance

If shyness is a series of choices, what is being chosen? It is a choice to be passive in verbal communications with other persons; it is a choice not to express feelings; it is a choice not to pay attention to other people; it is a choice to dwell on wishes, fantasies, and one's past or future rather than to pay attention to this moment. Paying attention to people becomes fearful and threatening to the shy person.

The opposite of shyness is choosing to be active. Being active means to be verbal in communication; it means expressing feelings; it means paying attention to other people; it means dwelling on reality instead of on fantasy.

A college basketball player who grew up in an Arizona resort community was talented, but he never lived up to his coach's expectation. During a game his mind was preoccupied either with mistakes he had made earlier or with ways to avoid mistakes in the future. He wondered if the coach was impressed with him or not. By being preoccupied with factors apart from the here and now, he became inhibited.

He lost his concentration. Since he did not perform automatically, he could not play as efficiently and as confidently as he should have. In most sports, to hesitate is to spoil the play.

To be active is to live in the present. To be passive is to be thinking about other times and other places.

Illusions of grandeur

Passivity results from the passionate wish to be somebody we know good and well we're not. The greater the discrepancy between what we wish we were and what we think we are, the greater the pathology of passivity.

22

As infants we have much to learn about life. Because of our limited capacities and experiences, our view is distorted. With the limited background and experience of infancy, we tend to believe that we are the center of our world. We come to the reasonable conclusion that mothers exist to satisfy our whims. We also conclude that we control our world in some magic way by our wishes. When we get hungry, we wish for relief. In some magic way, without our doing anything, food comes. When we're uncomfortable, we desire relief, and in some mystical way mother comes and changes our diapers. In most cases babies cannot act—they can only wish. Because of their dependency and helplessness, infants conclude: "If I wish hard enough, I will be taken care of and my world will be arranged. I do not have to do anything." This is common among infants of all societies.

As children develop their particular perspectives of the world, the distinction between wishes and reality is quite vague. Children spend a good deal of time, and gain a great deal of pleasure from, wishing. (In adults it is called "daydreaming.") Wishing is the opposite of being active toward one's environment.

When reality is disappointing, children enjoy thinking of wishes and the possibility that they might soon be fulfilled. This causes the anxiety or depression to go away for a while. Children wish to be famous athletes . . . adolescents wish to be rock stars or dancers . . . adults wish to be rich or wealthy or good looking—all these fantasies give pleasure by temporarily setting aside reality and offering the possibility that our wishes could come true.

"If only . . ."

Shy people, all 85 million of them, prefer to be passive and maintain their wishes rather than be active and risk being common or mediocre. Inevitably shy people believe if only ————, then people would ————. (You can fill in your own blanks in the previous sentence.)

The first part might be:	*The second part might be:*
If only I were beautiful	People would respect me
If only I were taller	People would pay attention to me
If only I were smarter	People would love me
If only I were a better conversationalist	People would worship me
If only I could tell jokes better	People would fall in love with me

Shy persons maintain a wish rather than face the grim reality that they are not what they want to be. Every time we come face to face with the fact that we're not what we want to be or are not being treated as we wish to be, we become angry. If, under the impact of reality, we change our impression of who we are or alter our wish to be treated in certain ways, we become depressed. Depression is the human psyche's response to loss. When we are forced to change the way we see ourselves, we feel a sense of loss. Parts of the old idealistic image are gone. This is why growing persons regularly experience mild and sometimes severe depression. The growing cycle is: We have a self-image; experience does not confirm it; we therefore alter our image. The result: growth.

This is a hard, maybe even cruel, view of the shy person's dilemma. But it is realistic. Admitting the place of fantasy in the inner life of self is a major step toward improvement.

The fundamental wish is the wish to be loved. Shy persons fantasize that if they remain passive and don't make any mistakes, they will be loved. "If I am active and aggressive in communication, I risk alienating people and being abandoned."

It is a world of "If only . . ." and it is a miserable mode of existence indeed.

2 | ON THE COUCH

> *What other dungeon is so dark as one's own heart! What jailer so inexorable as one's self!*
>
> NATHANIEL HAWTHORNE

As a counselor listens to thousands of clients, patterns begin to emerge which are common to all shy persons.

Loneliness

Floyd was an electronics wizard absorbed in a quest to build the finest high fidelity stereo unit. He spent most of his paycheck on perfecting his sound system and became quite animated while discussing his handiwork.

When friends came to his house, he expected them to be attentive to his latest adaptations. But when they began to talk about *their* projects Floyd was disinterested. When he lost the spotlight he felt threatened. Since no one was paying any attention to him he felt unloved, lonely, depressed.

Gradually the engineer turned more and more to his hi-fi for companionship. The stereo never disagreed, never threatened, always stopped when he turned off the switch.

In counseling sessions Floyd had to confront the reasons for his misery. He contended that he was "just naturally shy," but that was his cover. Therapy disclosed the real situation in vivid detail.

In his infancy, Floyd had formed a close attachment to his mother. She gave him her total attention. He adopted the view that the ideal world was one of an active, nurturing mother and a passive, receptive boy. Any situation which violated this vision led him to feel he was losing his relationship with his mother, hence losing his mother's love. He began to assume that his mother also wanted this idealized relationship.

As a result of his vision of the world he flunked out of several colleges, even though he had a brilliant mind. Classes which required only reading were fine. But if Floyd was asked to write a report or to recite orally, he could not complete the assignment. Writing or reciting was being active. If he became active, he moved away from the position of the passive, receptive boy and thus saw himself moving away from his mother's care.

Finally Floyd admitted that he did not want to grow up. He did not want to shoulder responsibility.

Only when he saw the true picture was he able to begin freeing himself from the shackles of passivity and dependency and enjoy deliverance from depression and loneliness.

Nelson, a 22-year-old bachelor, also knew the loneliness of the shy. He could send his 18-wheeler freight truck roaring over the highways, but he could not bring himself to enjoy the social companionship of women.

Because of the superficial interaction between Nelson and his mother, he idealized women, putting them on a pedestal and treating them as if they were fragile dolls to be protected from his own aggression. He became anxious, fawning, and syrupy sweet around the opposite sex.

When he recognized that his concept of motherly perfection was unrealistic and as he had more experience with females, he saw that women could be rough and tumble human beings—as hearty as males. As he became less concerned about his own behavior and the possibility of making errors, his crippling shyness began to fade.

Boredom

Shy people are frequently bored. When they say, "There's nothing to do," they are really saying, "My environment isn't stimulating me."

People become bored when they are afraid to become active toward their environment, afraid to apply their feelings to people, places, and things around them. Active, creative people can walk through an empty lot and see all kinds of bugs and flowers, shapes and sizes. But a person who is not going to give any value or feelings to things outside himself can be bored in the middle of a war. Why? Because shy persons don't pay attention to things outside themselves. Boredom is paying attention to things inside, not outside.

Boredom results from the fear of becoming active toward things outside and losing fantasies. When students complain that they're bored in school they are quick to blame the institution. But active pupils in their same classes are never bored. They have inquisitive minds. They'll read a book or draw pictures or write poetry. A mature person is seldom bored.

Rembrandt couldn't be bored anywhere because he saw beauty everywhere.

Victor Frankl, in a Nazi prison camp for three years, testified that he was not overcome with boredom.

Blaise Pascal, imprisoned as a monk, developed an entire new system of math in prison.

Boredom does not depend on the environment. It depends on how you allow yourself to feel about your environment.

Fear

The continuum of shyness extends from casual reluctance about talking to an irrational fear of being destroyed or of destroying others.

The fear of failure is prominent among shy people. This liability has some assets. It makes us try harder to succeed. Good public speakers testify that a measure of shyness forces them to prepare well for each lecture, lest they be embarrassed. Actually, fear of failure is not the real fear. The real fear is fear of being imperfect—fear of not living up to our unrealistic expectations of ourselves. Once we reduce our expectations we no longer are afraid of "failure."

Other shy people are torn by the dilemma:

> I *need people*
> I *want people*
> I *depend on people*
> I'm *afraid of people*

Because of their passivity, such people cannot make contact. Nearly every moment of their lives is spoiled by this very real fear of being less than "I ought to be."

Martyrdom

Shy people often live with a self-imposed martyrdom, a kind of masochism—they enjoy feeling lousy. A martyr personality chooses to remain passive and helpless for the purpose of getting other people to be active toward him or her.

"Other people have made me this way," they conclude. More accurately they are admitting, "If I am weak and suffering, then people will pay attention to me. If I start feeling strong, people won't give me special consideration." When people realize that they choose to feel martyrized as part of the desire to remain helpless infants, their responses toward other people greatly improve.

Imperfection

We used to think that inferiority complexes were real, that shy people actually felt terribly inferior. Through the process of listening to people talk for thousands of hours on the couch, we've come to realize that it's not comparison with other people that makes them depressed. The central problem is comparing themselves with perfection.

The clue to this is that people don't feel inferior in areas where they are really inferior. Bright people feel "dumb." The best cooks think the meal is inadequate. The most beautiful women are the most concerned about their looks. The accomplished musician is emotionally shattered by a single error.

The simple explanation that people feel inferior to other people does not explain such anxiety. An engineer might be inferior in music to most experienced musicians and feel almost no anxiety about it because he has accepted his position of inferiority in music. It is in the areas where he is *good* but wishes he were *perfect* that he is most bothered.

Strange as it may seem, shy people invariably wish to be charming, witty, attention-getting conversationalists. They are not satisfied merely to be paid attention to occasionally. Those who are most bothered by their shyness have the most unrealistic ideals of how they want people to treat them in social situations.

Bill, popular as a comedian, dominated most conversations. People enjoyed his wit. In therapy he complained that people didn't seem to respect him in group situations. With time he admitted that, in addition to being the center of attention, he wanted his ideas to be thoroughly respected. He wanted to be known as an intellectual. Because of his unrealistic wish for himself, he was not content merely to be the center of attention.

A collegian with a sprightly disposition—albeit rather bookish and limited in his interests—sought earnestly to increase his circle of friends. Nathan believed that people who were cheerful were loved, so he was all smiles all the time. He was puzzled when his overtures did not bring instant acceptance and flocks of friends.

Rather than bowling everyone over by his friendliness and gathering the applause he sought, he found that he was largely ignored. He realized that he was too possessive of other people—a bit too demanding of their attention. And he realized that occasionally anger would display itself. His constant smiles were a lie. He was not being authentic in his communications with others, and his discrepancies made people restless.

The years following college were good ones for

the "eager beaver." Nathan was loved supremely in his marriage; business associates gave him room to grow; he maintained a spiritual discipline. His shyness yielded to maturity and the outcome was a more rewarding and fulfilling life.

Would that all shy people were as fortunate.

A new perspective

Behavior stems from our understanding of the situation at the moment. We act according to the way we perceive ourselves and the world around us. Dr. Kurt Lewin, noted social psychologist, uses the term "life-space" to describe all the things we're paying attention to at any given moment, both outside and inside ourselves, including the way we feel. Most self-concepts include a concept of other people. Persons who see themselves as leaders see others as followers. Persons who see themselves as passive see others as being active toward them. Persons who see themselves as victims see others as perpetrators. Such perspectives may not be accurate.

Permanent changes of behavior occur only when people change their perspective of themselves and other people. Crash diets, stop-smoking schemes, and teetotaler programs bring only temporary results unless those involved alter their perspective of themselves and their world.

Successful behavior change involves a good deal of discussion with other persons and hearing other perspectives. The failure of New Year's resolutions is a standard joke. Unless we come to see the world in some significantly different way, we will resort to our old patterns of responding.

If a man enters a room and says to himself, "Everyone is watching me. I'd better do things properly," he'll have fear. He'll be inhibited or act awkwardly. As he comes to realize that indeed most people are not watching him and that other people don't look on errors as disasters, he will walk into a group situation with greater confidence. His inaccurate perception of the situation was based on his desire to be important, which made him think that people were watching him.

A woman who says to herself, "If I make a fool of myself people will laugh," will be very cautious about what she says. When she realizes that generally people are quite tolerant about errors, she will not be as concerned about what she says and will walk about with more confidence. It all depends on her perspective.

When shy persons change their perspective of themselves and others, shyness ceases to be a problem.

Note the wide disparity between the shy person's perspective and a more realistic perspective:

Shy person's perspective	Realistic perspective
1. I am a victim.	1. I contribute to my personality by my choices.

2. I would be more loved if I were less shy.

3. I'd be happier if I would be a better conversationalist.

4. I'm going to learn some jokes. Then I'll be the center of attention.

5. I don't want to be on top. I just want to get a little bit of attention.

6. I feel so inferior. It bothers me.

7. Some day they'll all respect me.

8. I feel in some way I'm bad or evil.

9. If I make mis-

2. I am loved now more than I'm willing to admit.

3. I really want to be a perfect conversationalist.

4. I'll never get as much attention as I want.

5. I want to be on top.

6. Anything less than perfection bothers me.

7. People will generally think about me as they do now.

8. I am no more bad or evil than anybody else.

9. If I make mis-

takes, people won't respect me.

takes, people will love me more, because I'm one of them.

10. If only I were better looking, I'd be more popular.

10. I'm better looking than I think I am.

11. If only I would be different, I'd be happier.

11. Happiness comes from accepting myself as I am, not how I wish I were.

Can shy people be helped?

Most shy people fight vigorously to maintain their present perspective on life. Really, they have no intention of growing out of their problems. Even though their current behavior is not fully satisfying, they are afraid to give up the wish of what they want to be for fear they will be totally alone. They want their feelings of greatness affirmed rather than altered.

What they want principally when they come into therapy is to dispel their bad feelings (have their wishes come true) without having to change their perspective. Change involves risks. And fear of risks prevents people from growing as rapidly as they could.

Mature perspectives

There is no one right way of seeing one's self in the world, but mature people have these perspectives in common:

1. I will never be perfect, but that's OK.

2. Nobody really owes me anything, and I don't owe them anything but to love them. As human beings we are all getting along in this world as best we can, but our success or failure in any given situation depends pretty much on us and nobody else.

3. I'm not omnipotent, but I'm strong enough to handle most situations. Those I can't handle I may mess up, but that's OK.

4. I will not be able to get any pure love from anybody. All human beings are to a greater or lesser degree wrapped up in themselves and cannot give me all the love I want. But that doesn't mean I'm totally alone.

5. I don't have to be the center of attention in order to be valuable. I will contribute where and when I can, and that's the best I should ever expect of myself.

3 | FIVE PROFILES OF THE SHY

*There are three kinds of people in
the world: wills, won'ts and can'ts.
The first accomplish everything;
the second oppose everything;
the third fail in everything.*
ECLECTIC MAGAZINE

No two shy people are alike. Behavior and personalities differ widely. In psychological terms we say shyness "spans a wide continuum."

The disorder lurks in the most unexpected personalities. Brash attorney Melvin Belli told Charlotte Beyers in *Parade* (Jan. 18, 1976) that he "became flamboyant to hide shyness."

An evangelist confided to his biographer that he rarely showed up in time for preliminaries because he was too shy to interact with people. Known for his magnificent pulpit delivery, he admitted that meeting people on a one-to-one basis terrified him.

Comedienne Phyllis Diller, quoted in *Family Circle* (February 1976), recalls that "teachers who knew me as a child told my parents I was the most painfully shy youngster they'd ever seen. I was so shy at school dances that I'd stay in the room with the coats. I was so afraid of making a noise at ball games I'd hum at yells."

The same issue of *Family Circle* tells that Roosevelt Grier, a mountain of a man who seemingly would fear nobody, went almost mute in school when laughed at for his size.

Barbara Walters, host for many years on the coast-to-coast NBC daily telecast *The Today Show,* was described by at least one associate as "aloof . . . cold . . . rude." But the popular interviewer explained her behavior in a newspaper feature by Christina Kirk published in the *Washington Star:*

> I have a slight inferiority complex still. I go into a room and have to talk myself into going up to people. . . . I can't take a vacation alone, eat in a restaurant alone. . . . I'm always hurt if someone says, "She's aggressive. . . ." If *I'm* the epitome of a woman who is always confident and in control, don't ever believe it of anyone.

Five basic classifications can be pinned on recruits of the shy troops: Shy-Dependent, Shy-Aggressive, Shy-Terrified, Shy-Anxious, and Shy-Contented. There is a good deal of overlap between these categories. Probably nobody fits into one category exclusively. If you spot yourself passing in review among these five divisions, report for duty at the changing of the guard and let the High Command know that a transformed soldier has joined the ranks.

Shy-dependent

Most timid persons come closest to this first category. Shy-dependent people generally are helpful, cooperative, and kind. They rarely show anger. When people describe them, they say: "He's nice, but I don't know much about him," or "She's good, but not very noticeable." They appear to be generally uninteresting people who rarely express opinions, feelings, or their own thinking in a firm or aggressive manner.

People who are shy-dependent see themselves as helpless infants and others as strong and capable. Their passivity and apparent helplessness are unconscious techniques to force others to take care of them, to protect them, to advise them, and to comfort them.

These people feel most comfortable in the strong mother and helpless child relationship. They are often good "mothers" to young children and to injured or crippled persons and animals. They enjoy playing the role of Good Samaritan as much as they enjoy the role of the helpless.

People in this category never move far from their comfortable, passive role. To act assertively by expressing an opinion or by sharing a feeling or by being responsible would be to lose their position as helpless children. Other people might no longer act as their strong protectors. They are assertive only in their fantasies. Outwardly they remain passive in order to cling to the hope that their fantasies might someday be fulfilled.

Bruce was a classic shy-dependent. Raised by his mother, a grandmother, and an aunt (each competing to see who could be the best "mother" to him), he developed extreme passive tendencies. Bruce wanted the whole world to treat him as his maternal trio had.

Eventually Bruce was married, but he remained passive. His wife disciplined the children, ran the home, and spent the money. His corporation told him what time to show up for work, what jobs to do, and whom to salute, so to speak.

His wife was patient until their three daughters were in their teen years. Then her patience dissolved. She threatened divorce, but still Bruce remained the quiet listener, the nonaggressive lover, the silent wallflower at parties, moving through life behind a mask that read: "That's just the way I am."

Although a Christian, Bruce was passive about those portions of the Bible which admonished him to provide leadership for his family. He would try occasionally to lead. Because his efforts at leadership were so painful, Bruce felt he was sacrificially attempting to conform to the biblical standards. Observers of the situation, however, saw him as almost a nonentity within the family unit.

His wife threatened to leave him unless he gave

her more support and acted more assertively toward her and the children. In spite of this threat, Bruce remained passive. He took the attitude, "It will work out." He could not see how his shyness was causing his wife's frustration. He was simply behaving in the way he had behaved toward all women all his life. He didn't understand that he was asking his wife to act like his mother rather than his wife. She wanted a husband, not a son.

When Bruce was forced into being assertive, he became angry and depressed because he feared losing his position as a passive-dependent child. To avoid these situations Bruce remained a nice, quiet, reliable guy . . . neither friendly nor unfriendly, and rather invisible in social situations. He did his work well and experienced little anxiety because he was able to maintain his passive position both at home and at work.

We terminated therapy for Bruce because he wasn't motivated to change. On the final day of therapy he expressed the fantasy that if his wife did indeed leave him, he could go back and live with his mother, aunt, and grandmother, which probably was what he wanted all along.

A lot of shy people are like Bruce—uninvolved. They appear placid and agreeable, but they are only placid and agreeable when they are allowed to remain uninvolved. When they are expected to perform, a torrent of anxiety, fear, and anger is released. They immediately do things that are designed to get them out of the active position. They cry, complain of illness, leave the room, or get others to talk or make jokes.

While aggressive children get the attention, shy-dependent youngsters offer few hints about their agonies. Only a shrewd and observant adult can spot the clues. Watch for comments like: "He just sits there all day," "She shows very few emotional reactions," "She seems so calm," or "He's such a good boy."

Parents and teachers like their children to be calm, conforming, and "good," but too much pliability in a child may lead to pathology. Adults need to help such children overcome their fear of being themselves, encouraging them to interact with their environment so they have a chance to alter their perspective of the world.

Children who do express their feelings, sometimes violently, get attention from parents, children, teachers, police officers, and government officials. We tend to think disturbed children are those who express themselves and make a nuisance of themselves, contradicting and fighting society. This is not necessarily true.

Many passive-dependent children grow up with an unreal perspective of themselves and the world. They seldom interact, so their unrealistic view of themselves is never tested or challenged. They remain dependent and ungratified in their relations with people. This is the great tragedy of the shy-dependent child.

"Billy is such a good child. He's never stolen anything, never taken drugs. . . ." We often hear this among parents of the shy-dependent child. But absence of delinquent behavior is not an adequate standard to judge the quality of a child's character. Dependent children may not act immorally, but neither do they act morally or develop strength of character. They are afraid to stand up for what they believe is right or to hold any firm opinions of their own.

Shy-dependent persons, though conforming, do not contribute to society and are not living a satisfying life. They suffer a good deal because of their shy behavior and their perspective of the world.

Shy-aggressive

This label may seem to present a contradiction. In clinical psychology this category is identified more commonly as the passive-aggressive personality. These people manipulate others with a shy-passivity that stems from a fear of being manipulated and ultimately a fear of being unloved. They are passive and shy in order to control and avoid being manipulated. They know that their shyness in certain situations is an irritant to other people and they tend to come away from such situations with a sense of smug victory. It's as if they're saying, "Aha! I won because you weren't able to dominate me." Life becomes Me versus Them. They have a strong need to ward off

the aggression of other people, and they are successful because of their passivity.

Listen to this candid comment from a shy-aggressive person in the clinic: "When people come at me
strong I just sit there and don't pay attention to what
they're saying. With a very passive expression on my
face, I let them rant and rave, and I feel very, very
smug."

Shy-aggressive persons will not allow themselves
to feel needy or loving toward others. Feeling needy
makes them feel weak. If shy-aggressive persons allow themselves to love, they feel the beloved has
power over them. When others have something shy-
aggressive persons want (love), others are seen as
powerful. Rather than allow themselves to feel love
toward others, shy-aggressives deny those feelings.
To them life is a power struggle. They must maintain the position of power. By forcing other people
to need them and by denying their need of other
people, shy-aggressive persons remain on the throne.

Herman, an accountant in a suburban office, illus-
trates the syndrome perfectly. He continually frus-
trates his wife, Shirley, but is unaware of his subtle
motives. Arriving home from the office, he immediately begins to read the evening paper. Shirley tries
to get through the barrier by initiating simple conversation, but Herman merely grunts his response.
After that routine continues awhile, Shirley becomes
exasperated and gives up trying to engage in conversation. She leaves the room and continues chores.

Herman complains, "Well, I've tried, but she gets mad and I can't converse with her." In this way he justifies his passivity, putting the blame on his wife and refusing to deal actively with her desire for even a little show of love and companionship. That is Herman's way of passively-aggressively avoiding the issue of Shirley's feelings. It makes him superior— even smug. He sees a world out to manipulate him by making him feel needy. And he sees his task as avoiding manipulation.

Whenever passive-aggressive persons believe they are being manipulated, they feel an immense loss of identity. Sometimes they parade a cocky superiority. At other times they are extremely quiet, saying just enough to irritate the person or cleverly to miss the point of a conversation. They tune out criticism against themselves and thus "win" each confrontation. By avoiding their own tender feelings, they maintain their position of power. These people are shy only in situations involving their tender feelings. They would rather fight than love.

A good example of the shy-aggressive in the New Testament is the young man in Jesus' parable who gladly responded to his father's command to work in the vineyard but never went out to report for duty.

Mother calls to her son, "Johnny, take out the garbage."

"Oh, right away, Mom," he replies. But two hours later it's not done. The boy is being cooperative on the surface but underneath he is saying, "I don't want to and you can't make me."

There is really only one way to deal with the shy-aggressive in the clinic. We provide an atmosphere where it is safe for the person's aggression to show and present no aggression of our own toward the client. We simply remain extremely passive and let the person slowly feel more and more able to deal with his or her own aggression and tender feelings without the threat of reciprocal aggression.

During initial stages of therapy, shy-aggressives want very much for the therapist to take an active role. They want to dominate the situation as they've been doing since childhood. They achieve dominance by encouraging other people to be aggressive, then frustrating them with passivity. Passive-aggressive persons become extremely angry in the initial stages of therapy when the therapist continues to remain passive. They angrily charge, "You're not helping me! You're not doing what I'm paying you for! I came here for advice and you're not doing anything."

A therapist's role during the early stages is to help such persons become aware of their feelings and motives. After a while they begin to see that their passive-aggression has been a life-long pattern. Slowly they realize that they have deliberately chosen this passive technique to ward off their own tender feelings. During the middle stages of therapy they recognize that their fear of other people's aggression is indeed exaggerated. They acknowledge that *they are* aggressive and angry, and that they have merely projected those feelings onto other people. Generally therapy with passive-aggressive persons is quite successful. They begin to see other people from a different perspective.

During the final stages of therapy, shy-aggressive persons begin to realize that what they wanted in life was to be loved unconditionally. Their anger developed because they were never loved unconditionally, but somehow had to earn the other person's love. As they realize this and see themselves and other people differently, passive-aggressive persons are more willing to be active, more willing to risk making mistakes, more willing to elicit other people's aggression and to experience their own tender feelings.

Shy-terrified

The shy people whose world is most distorted are those who live in constant terror of their own rage and of other people's rage toward them. They withdraw almost totally from society, preferring to live in their own fantasies. They can tolerate little social contact and then they withdraw either geographically or mentally.

Their profoundest wish is to be held by a perfect mother or father and cuddled forever. Since every situation falls short of this fantasy, they are in constant rage because their wishes are not being fulfilled. To guard themselves against such terribly unpleasant feelings, they withdraw from people.

Their behavior is called "shyness." They much prefer living in their gratifying fantasies to interacting with persons who do not give them the cuddling they need. They are often known as eccentric, peculiar, reclusive, or (in extreme cases) hermits.

In social situations, as their wishes are constantly frustrated, their rage climbs to the point where they are in terror of exploding with violent behavior. If they were to put words to their feelings, they would say, "I could kill everyone in this room!" or "I could blow up the whole world!" or "If I had a gun, I'd put everyone to death!" To avoid such actions, they simply deny their rage and withdraw.

Occasionally shy-terrified people explode in dramatic activities which garner headlines in the newspapers. The media routinely carry stories of the shy-terrified person who opens fire on innocent victims or who murders parents, neighbors, and perhaps even strangers. But usually such persons are able to control their rage.

Most often the shy-terrified does not recognize this inner rage. Clues are the following:

• Afraid of others, the shy-terrified usually deny their own rage by assuming it is the other people who are angry.

• They fantasize about being comforted, held, and cuddled.

• Sometimes they feel as if they're likely to do great violence to themselves and other people.

• They find themselves wanting to withdraw from

people and not being able to pay attention to others, even though they try.

Bob was 29 before he sought help for his shyness. Friends excused him. "You know Bob. He's so shy he hardly ever comes to our activities. And when he does, he stays to himself."

Bob would stand in the back of a group rather than sit on a chair with the rest. His therapy sessions revealed many and varied fantasies. One which he relished was buying a gun and shooting people at random. His imagination so frightened him that he was eager and ready for therapy.

Today Bob understands why he is shy, and he is able to face his rage and control it. He's dating, joining in group activity, and working out of his fantasies.

"I don't have to shoot people," he said after two and a half years of therapy. "I can feel my rage, but now I understand it. And since I can see where it's coming from, I seem to have the power to reduce its effect on me."

On August 1, 1966, Charles Joseph Whitman climbed a tower at the University of Texas in Austin and opened fire on citizens below. At the end of his shooting spree, 16 people were dead and 25 wounded.

Whitman had been an Eagle Scout, a concert pianist, and a model husband and father. After the tragedy friends remembered that he had told them repeatedly that he was thinking of climbing the tower and shooting people with a deer rifle. At age

25, "the thinker," Charlie Whitman, could no longer outrun his rage. He performed the unthinkable violence of his imagination and paid for it with his death—and with the death of his pretty wife, who was the first victim of his bullets that dreadful afternoon.

A young man 18 years of age strangled a 7-year-old girl in a New York church. He was known to his friends as unemotional and had made plans to become a minister.

In Phoenix, a polite, soft-spoken 11-year-old boy stabbed his brother 34 times.

The shy-terrified most often have had severe disturbances in their early childhood and need to seek professional help over a long period to work through their distorted representation, feelings, and fears about themselves and other people.

Shy-anxious

Hand-wringing is a typical manifestation of this problem among the ranks of the shy. Shy-anxious persons have a great deal of difficulty getting into prolonged or deep conversations with people. They spend their time flitting from one situation to the next.

Many good hostesses are shy-anxious women who use their hospitality to keep loneliness at bay and themselves in a whirl of activity. Intimacy eludes them. They appear to be vivacious and extroverted, but inside they are terrified of deep involvements.

Their relationships are superficial and shallow. When asked to express an opinion on a current event or situation, they giggle or respond with a frivolous remark and go on their way.

The shy-anxious male might be a comedian or a good storyteller. Sometimes he appears to be a bully. He may be a flashy dresser who wears fancy rings and has tendencies toward exhibitionism, driving flashy cars, and smoking cigars.

In clinical psychology shy-anxious people are known as hysterical personalities—persons who are afraid to see themselves as they really are. They generally fear becoming truly male or female. Masculine or feminine aggression in sexuality is something they have never accepted in themselves. They have a profound fear that expression of sexuality or aggression is bad and will lead to disapproval by parents. Forever fixed at puberty, they are afraid to move through adolescence and adulthood, recognizing that feelings of sexuality are normal and healthy. They are perpetual junior-highers, with all the accompanying exhibitionism, fadism, and rapid fluctuations of emotions. They fear responsibility and commitment.

Shy-anxious people cling to a fantasy of themselves as being perfect, because if they achieve anything less than perfection, they feel worthless. They're unable to accept the middle ground between totally good and totally bad. They are likely to be labeled "conceited," since sometimes they believe the myth that they are as perfect as they wish to be.

Shy-anxious people have an abundance of nervous energy. They talk fast, move fast, twitch, and bob their feet. The devout often carry a Bible or other symbols of devotion. They are always looking for support for their fantasies about their own moral uprightness, and they tend to deny evidence to the contrary.

Naturally they can't get involved with people. Others might find some imperfection in them. They keep running to avoid any hint of imperfection. "I'm good," they repeat, turning away from any situation in which they might obviously fail. They sense they are weak and imperfect, but to acknowledge this consciously would crush their fantasies.

Doris was a charmer in a lavish suburban home where all her friends admired her as a wonder woman. She was an engaging hostess, had children in college, and enjoyed success in sales. When she put her energy and planning into gear, things got done.

But behind her front door, Doris was another person—tired most of the time, lonely, discouraged. She kept her relationships with people superficial. If a friendship approached intimacy, she feared her guard would drop and she would say and do things displaying her sexual or aggressive tendencies. Conversing with her was like trying to catch a bird. As soon as anyone got close, she flew away. Most people wouldn't have classified her as shy, yet she was afraid to be active toward others. She needed love and caring, but she worked against achieving it.

In therapy sessions, a torrent of anger flowed from this "super" woman. A year and a half passed before Doris would allow herself the liberty to name her "sins" and not be crushed by them.

People such as Doris light cigarettes and don't smoke them. They carry a drink around at a party and only take a sip. Cigarettes and drinks serve as barriers. Rings and lipstick may also be used as barriers. When shy-anxious women come in for their first counseling session, the barriers are all there— long eyelashes, heavy mascara, fresh lipstick. They are saying, "Everything's great. Just don't get beyond this mask."

Many Christian churches and homes foster this type of anxiety by convincing people that achieving the ideal life is not only possible but probable. Ministers and teachers who need to deny their own imperfections subtly or openly imply that their lives consist of unending victories over anxiety, depression, and other bad feelings. By implying that their own lives are relatively perfect, they encourage their listeners to see themselves in the same way. So people deny their imperfections and the realities of their personalities.

Motives are rarely pure. They are nearly always contaminated by a certain amount of selfishness and narcissism. Recognizing this keeps us from overrating ourselves and helps us accept other people's weaknesses.

Shy-anxious persons need to recognize that although they are not OK, they are loved by God and by other people.

Shy-contented

Not all shy people are dependent, aggressive, terrified, or anxious. Some merely withdraw without suffering the usual telltale emotions. Their shyness is not a problem to them. When called upon, they can relate to people naturally. But they simply prefer activities they can do alone. Their shyness is perfectly acceptable. They are the shy-contented.

Shy-dependent persons are afraid to move away from being cuddled.

Shy-aggressive persons must manipulate people.

Shy-terrified persons keep a lock on their rage.

Shy-anxious persons remain aloof, lest they lose their masks.

None of the above describes the shy-contented. These people function well. They carry on their activities, sometimes doing things that leaders could not sit still long enough to accomplish. Being active toward people does not cause them discomfort and they don't cause other people problems. Shyness is only an occasional problem. They have no critical need for alteration.

If you fall into the shy-contented category and life is relatively pleasant for you and those around you,

you need not spend time or energy attempting to change.

Summary

Shy behavior is not automatically pathological. It is pathological only if it accompanies unpleasant feelings, bad relationships, and harmful behavior.

Sufferers in the first four categories have no easy answers or gimmicks for change. An evangelist's easy steps to maturity or keys to better living may be superficial. The *person* has to change. That's the longest, hardest route to maturity, but it's the only valid one.

We live in a pragmatic society. Our highest praise is reserved for the inventor or the pioneer who carves out a stake in the wilderness and clears land for a farm. The ideal American is self-made. Unfortunately, we bring this same mind-set to our psychological problems. We treat mental ills in the same concrete fashion. The way to get a farm is simply to buy 10 acres, chop down the trees, and plant corn. The way to solve a problem in marriage is to touch bases one, two, and three. Not so!

The fly in the ointment is that the solution to the problem is determined by how we understand the problem. Insisting on simple solutions for complex problems eventually complicates the remedy. This the shy person must understand. Sometimes the road to recovery is long and hard. But there are ways to resolve problems. The next chapters show how.

4 | HOW TO HELP A SHY CHILD

Let a child venture. The mistakes of children are often better than their no-mistakes.

H. W. BEECHER

The air was cool as Marcia shuffled along in the twilight over the disintegrating sidewalk to her house. But she didn't notice the night air creeping in. The 10-year-old girl made herself warm by thinking how snug she would be when her doctor and his wife would come to adopt her. "They don't have a little girl," she said aloud. "So they'll come and take me to live in their big house."

But when Marcia arrived at the corner of Mason and Clearwater, there was no doctor, only the blue Chevy of her mother's boyfriend parked at the curb. A light was on upstairs. Anger, disappointment, and feelings of worthlessness churned within her.

Marcia let herself into the house and made her

57

way to the kitchen. "Tonight I'll be adopted," she murmured to herself, as she did each evening. "Somebody will love me and give me a home."

She selected a new jar of peanut butter from the pantry and made a sandwich, then curled up in a chair to munch a withered apple. Her mother called from upstairs to see if she was home. The man in the blue Chevy left. *If my doctor doesn't come soon to adopt me, I'll be asleep,* Marcia thought. Darkness fell on the little house.

From birth Marcia had been neglected. An illegitimate child, she had no stabilizing influence of a father. Totally ignored, she built her dreams around the day when someone would give her the security of a family.

At 30, Marcia is still wishing. She cannot understand why others haven't taken her into their family. The real world has been cruel, so the shy-terrified, still a child, has created an imaginary world into which she frequently escapes.

When Marcia is with people she does her best to be charming and warm. But anger which she experienced in her childhood grows so intense that after an hour in social situations she begins to develop fantasies about killing everyone. She tries to avoid such feelings by escaping into her world of fantasy. Her friends ask, "Marcia, are you with us?" or "Marcia, you seem bored." She passes these off with a casual, "I'm OK," but rage is boiling inside. At last she must withdraw from the group lest she shatter her world of respectability by uncontrolled violence. Offering some pretense, she goes somewhere by herself and fantasizes about an elusive world with mother and father and a protective home in which her tattered emotions can be made whole.

Marcia is shy because of the way she was treated by her lonely, frustrated mother and because of the concept of her world she developed as a child. Other children in the same environment might have developed different fantasies and fears, but clearly Marcia's shyness grew out of her deprived background. What about shy, hurting persons who grew up in relatively happy families?

Shyness from conception

The specific mechanisms of heredity are not well understood, but it seems probable that genetic factors predispose some persons to shyness. Two children, raised in identical environments, can develop differing degrees and kinds of shyness, due to hereditary dispositions.

Children contribute a great deal both to their environment and to their development. A newborn infant whose inherited disposition is active and inquisitive is going to get more positive responses from the environment than an infant who is genetically more passive. A child who, because of heredity, has greater physiological responses to emotional situations, lives in a different world than the child whose glands secrete less under emotional stimuli.

Our current knowledge of genetic influences on behavior is too simplistic for us to determine whether behavior is caused by heredity or environment. Undoubtedly shyness can be partly attributed to genetics. It seems equally apparent that environment has a large influence in the development of shyness. Within the parameters established by genetic factors, children become shy to a greater or lesser degree depending on their interactions with people, especially parents.

Let's look at parental behavior which contributes to the development of shyness in children.

Shy parents

Parents who are shy often have some shy children. This does not imply that shyness is copied, imitated, or inherited. It is passed along through a complex set of personality factors. The chief one is parents' anxiety over expressions of emotion. When a child expresses emotion—for example, anger—shy parents feel threatened. They can't tolerate having their own emotions brought out. Shy parents who are afraid of being active and want to remain passive become anxious. So rather than pay attention to the child's problem, they fight to conceal their own emotions.

Since shy parents tend to reject their children in emotional situations, the children learn that having an emotion is bad. When they do have emotions, they conclude they are bad as persons, and they fear being unloved. To avoid letting their badness show, they refrain from talking, avoid conversations (except superficial ones), and develop shy behavior.

Shy parents continually stifle their children's feelings. They would rather passively dwell in their own thoughts than actively interact with their children. As a result, conversation is minimal and children quickly learn that quietness is the right way to live; conversation is out of place.

Fathers who are shy often wonder why their children are not free and comfortable in their presence. These fathers are sincerely hurt because they feel unloved by their own children. They usually are not able to realize that their own anxiety about interaction is communicated to the children and hence the children feel uncomfortable and reluctant to talk. These fathers truly love their children but are unable to overcome their own fear of being active.

Families that have fathers of this type often sit around evenings doing essentially nothing and communicate very little. Each member of the family is crying for attention, love, and companionship, but their anxiety is too great to risk interaction and each lives in his or her isolated world.

Neglectful parents

Millions of children with both parents present in their home still have no one who pays attention to their needs, fears, and desires. Many homes are materially well off, medically provided for, and nutritionally overindulged, but have little interaction.

Children whose parents are afraid of intimacy are not much better off than a child who has no parents at all. They will grow up believing that they are all alone in the world and that nobody cares about their needs. In their early years they will not learn adequate ways of relating to and communicating with people. Throughout life they will feel inadequate and simply withdraw from any unstructured conversations with other persons.

Betty was abandoned by her mother during the first six months of her life and spent her early years going from one foster home to another. At age eight she was taken in by a Christian family who did as much as they could for Betty, but her perspective of the world was that nobody would ever stay with her and nobody was to be trusted.

She is now married and her husband is complaining that she doesn't believe him when he says he loves her. She is afraid to enjoy the loving attention of her husband. His devotion makes her tense. Unconsciously she believes that if she loves him fully he will be so overwhelmed by her dependencies that he too will abandon her.

Each time they become intimate she pulls back and grows cold, aloof, and actually hostile. Because she was neglected as a baby, Betty is having extreme difficulty relating to other people on anything but a businesslike manner.

Busy parents who have exciting, demanding careers may unknowingly contribute to painful shyness in their offspring. If mother and dad don't pay attention to their children's mud pies, caterpillars, dolls, and butterflies, the children will learn that their ideas, interests, and emotions are of no value, and that there are more important things in life than their needs. Consequently the children will give little value to themselves or other people.

Smothering parents

Another common type of parents associated with the development of shyness is mothers and fathers who "smother" their children. This is especially common among mothers who attach themselves too closely to their offspring, counting on the success of their children to provide emotional gratification for themselves. They are overly involved in the children's lives, using subtle ways to keep the children dependent and childlike. Each time the child hints at independence, the mother tries to make the child feel naughty for leaving her alone.

Children seek to sustain the original warm relationship with mother, so they avoid becoming independent and remain subdued and bashful. They grow up seeing themselves essentially as extensions of the parent's personality rather than clearly separated individuals.

Overly strict parents

Shy children come most often from overly strict homes. Their parents see raising children as a power struggle. In the clinic such parents complain that their children keep trying to assert their independence or to get away with things, or that their children have stubborn wills which need to be broken.

Through therapy these parents come to realize that they feel somewhat weak and impotent and consequently are easily threatened. They see their children as powerful enemies who must be kept subdued at all times.

The children of strict parents see their father as a terrifying monster who must be pampered. As a result, conversations with him become guarded. Boys have a difficult time identifying with overly strict fathers. They tend to cling to their mothers and are unlikely to develop normal strength and power. To be aggressive would be to do battle with father and leave the security of mother, so they repress their own aggressiveness.

Children who feel little warmth from either parent will turn away from both parents and create ideal fantasy parents to whom they can run when they are anxious. These children will not be able to have deep feelings for anybody, even though superficially they will be attractive, pleasant people.

When overly strict parents recognize their fears and their struggle for power, they begin to relax. This in turn frees the children to experience and express their own feelings of all kinds—aggressive and tender. Their shyness will diminish.

Parents and adolescents

Adults, when asked about their toughest years, generally select the years from ages 12 to 14. For a child who is shy, these are years of total misery. Adolescents are attempting to break further away from parental domination. As a result of their self-imposed alienation from their parents, they cling tenaciously to peers for security and support. The more difficult the parents are to relate to, the closer the young people draw to their peers.

To avoid the depression and anxiety that accompany breaking away from home, adolescents resort to all kinds of activities including athletics, delinquencies, intensive study, and parties, perhaps with alcohol and drugs. All of these are ways of escaping unpleasant feelings which accompany this period of identity formation and independence seeking.

Parents who fail to see this period for what it is feel a tremendous loss of power and influence over their children. They get visions of their children becoming criminals or delinquents and they feel they have failed as parents. As a result, they reject their teenagers. Some go as far as turning them over to juvenile authorities.

We have seen many homes in which an unbridgeable chasm has developed between parents and their teenagers. When parents are able to recognize that their children's intense striving for identity and independence is relatively temporary, their relationship with their children can be improved. Understanding diffuses emotions, and families interact less destructively.

Pimples, scars, various inadequacies or imagined inadequacies of nature add fuel to the raging fires of shyness within the bashful teenager. An ounce of peer influence at this stage weighs more than a pound of parental guidance. Mother can nag her boy for half a decade to comb his hair, but one word from a girl about how nice his hair looks groomed will put a comb in his pocket for keeps.

The antisocial behavior of teenagers is often a compensation for problems related to shyness. That's why children who are quiet and conforming in elementary years often leap headlong into delinquency, vandalism, and cocky behavior as teenagers. They're trying to compensate for deep feelings of imperfection. Delinquency is an adolescent's way of saying, "I'm somebody. I don't need you. I don't need society. I can take care of myself. And if you criticize me or try to stop me, you're my enemy."

Behind such bravado often are teenagers who are striving hard to live up to their own ideals about themselves but who are very much afraid. They cling to any group offering status. The group may be comprised of people whose common desire is to be hostile toward parents.

These who turn so suddenly into delinquents at puberty can just as suddenly outgrow the stage and become conforming adults.

Ways to diminish shyness in children

Being a parent helps most people grow up. Others just grow old. Whether parents are growers or just agers depends on their perspective.

Some parents adopt the philosophy that they are doomed to remain as they are for the rest of their lives. If they hold to this way of thinking, it will become a self-fulfilling prophecy. Other parents see life as an opportunity for growth and maturation. They see challenges and other sources of anxiety as opportunities for growth. This too will become self-fulfilling.

If parents need to feel essentially perfect, if they cannot tolerate seeing inadequacies and immaturity in themselves, they will not be growing, exciting individuals. They will tend rather to be rigid, narrow, and self-centered. Such parents try to convince their children that fate is the prime developer of personality and that they have no control over who they are and how they develop. Parents who are growers, on the other hand, will be self-reflective and will change. Their children will note these changes and will have the perspective that growth is not only possible but probable and good. The impact of parents on their children is not infinite by any means, but it is great.

Suggestions for parents

As a capsule summary for parents or for those working with children and adolescents who have a problem with shyness, we have distilled the following suggestions from our knowledge of biblical and psychological principles:

1. Know yourself. Work out your own personal perspective of yourself and the world in a realistic fashion. See this self-perspective as a constantly changing panorama rather than a fixed photograph.

2. If you are living with your spouse, communicate honestly, openly, and continuously about yourself and your understanding of your spouse. The cardinal rule of communication between husband and wife is:

> We listen to understand the other;
> We talk to understand ourselves.

Too often our listening and talking to our spouse is for the purpose of altering him or her. Too often we think that our joy and contentedness depend on the other, and hence we try to manipulate and change the other for our own gratification. This inevitably is destructive to the marriage relationship and is destructive to the children.

Single parents or those whose spouses are not mature enough to handle discussion must find a safe friend to share with, someone mature enough to provide freedom and objectivity without threatening the relationship.

3. Pay attention to your child's wishes, feelings, and desires. Children need to feel that they are important. They need someone to notice their ideas

and feelings and expressions. Children should not, of course, be indulged in all their wishes, choices, and fears, but they do need to be understood. If their parents listen when they talk about scraped knees and pollywogs and tricycles, children learn that they are valuable and they develop confidence in speaking with others.

4. Be free in giving compliments. Honest expression of approval is helpful to both children and adults. When we mention this to some parents, their first response is, "We don't want Jane to become conceited so we don't tell her when she does well or looks good."

In fact, compliments have just the opposite effect. Conceit and self-centeredness develop in people who feel inadequate, inferior, and insecure. People who are not complimented or who are insulted develop fantasies about their greatness and form exalted opinions of themselves. Persons who are reasonably complimented are free to gain more realistic views of themselves.

It is impossible to compliment a person too much. Compliments create problems only when they are given for the purpose of motivating or manipulating the other person for selfish purposes. When we give compliments to get compliments or when we give compliments to make the other person feel obligated, then the compliments are damaging. But a genuine compliment can only be helpful to our children, to our spouses, or to other human beings.

5. Develop the perspective that feelings are neither good nor bad per se. Joy, pleasure, anger, grief, depression, and anxiety do not have any moral quality and will continue to be normal human responses. The Bible never condemns feelings. Destructive fantasies and behavior are condemned, but feelings are not.

Every feeling that can lead to destruction can also lead to good. Anger can kill, but it can also be channeled into highly productive service—study, writing, teaching. Fear, which can shackle, can also be turned into an invention to save lives or make the world more livable.

Parents who assure their children that feelings are OK help their children build self-confidence. On that foundation children can build respect and love for other people because they respect themselves.

6. Spend time on a regular basis in conversation with your children. It is not the quantity but the quality of time that is important. A half hour of pleasant conversation at dinner is much better than two hours of arguing or bickering. Parents must resist substituting entertainment for conversation. Families who do not converse together grow perverse together.

A father once brought his teenage daughter into our office, complaining that the girl was beyond his control, disrespectful, and a drug addict.

"She's out to destroy herself," he said, ending his tirade.

The 17-year-old girl sat calmly with grim face.

When she could speak, she said in a strained but modulated voice, "Dad, I've been trying to tell you for a year that I've stopped using drugs. One of my best friends died from an overdose and I quit immediately."

The girl went on to relate how she had become part of an antidrug poster campaign at school and was known as one of the "straights" because of her antidrug position. This had been going on for months, but the father was so confirmed in his anger that he wouldn't sit down and talk with his somewhat reformed daughter.

Kids can handle current problems, too. If dad loses his job or feels depressed or angry, they can deal with that information. Children are usually more realistic and optimistic than adults.

7. Don't dwell on your child's shyness. Most parents want to know if they should bring up the subject. In all problems, the children should set the pace for discussion. Parents can bring up the issue occasionally just to let their youngster know they are aware of it, but they shouldn't push for detailed conversation until the child is ready and brings it up first.

8. See the child as a total person. Too often defects such as shyness begin to dominate our view of who the child is. Many strong points are forgotten.

It's very comforting to children to know that things they say at a given moment do not represent the totality of their thinking and feeling and won't be held against them. Children can make some rather wild statements occasionally and parents should not see this either as a trend or something that is fixed in concrete. Very often children say things they don't really believe. They are merely sampling new ideas and testing their parents' love. Your child is far from what he or she is going to become. Children, especially teenagers, have radical thoughts and feelings, but the great majority of children revert to the standards and attitudes of the home in which they grew up.

9. Let children know that all their friends are welcome at your house. If you're home, accept these friends with good spirits. An open front door supports the shy teen, builds self-esteem, and encourages peer acceptance. Provide snacks and let the gang have privacy and music.

10. Share with your children your own shy experiences in the good ol' days. Young people have a somewhat mystical view of adulthood. To them it's a world of achievement and total control. When children understand that their parents have struggled and are struggling with feelings of inadequacy, passivity, and shyness, they take courage.

11. Present a healthy attitude toward sexuality. Relationships with the opposite sex are critical, especially during adolescent years. The views of sexuality they develop during childhood influence people greatly.

The more openly affectionate parents can be, the more mature will be the attitude of their children.

If adolescents are free to talk about boy friends or girl friends and dating, they will have a much healthier attitude toward the opposite sex. Encourage moral behavior and discourage acting out of sexual behavior, but allow adolescents to verbalize feelings.

12. Don't look on shyness as "the plague." If parents try to identify with their "suffering child," and are bothered by suffering they imagine their child is enduring, they strengthen the grip of shyness.

Parents do not have total control over the development of shyness in their children. But interaction of parents and children from birth on is very important and does a great deal to determine the degree of shyness or freedom from shyness that children will experience throughout their adult lives.

Summary

For shy children there is no sure path through these troubled waters. Raging emotions wash out bridges, smash down communication lines, and erode peaceful valleys where they could have dwelled in reasonable tranquility. But communication between parents and children is essential. Aim to spend a half hour each day with each child. It is good for both boys and girls to have time alone with each parent individually. Girls like to have dates with their dad. Go to a coffee shop together and have fun listening and sharing. Sons find perspective from their mom concerning female feelings. Both sons and daughters are watching and learning.

5 | IF YOU'RE SINGLE AND SHY

*Shy she was,
and I thought her cold.*
ALFRED LORD TENNYSON

People are single for many reasons: death of spouse, divorce, a desire for freedom, to make time for a cause, dedication to a career, neurotic fear of intimacy, unrealistic expectations of the opposite sex, and unattractive physical and psychological traits. A single life is not a disaster or a tragedy. Many single persons live full, rich, rewarding lives. They are able to have deep, gratifying friendships. Generally persons who are happily married will be happily single.

Some are single because of their shyness with the opposite sex. Many of these people feel frustrated and anxious. Life is often seen as hopeless and without pleasure. This chapter is for singles who want to improve their relationships with the opposite sex.

Vexed by the opposite sex

Inevitably persons who are especially shy around the opposite sex see them as powerful, desirable, necessary, and rejecting. A healthy relationship consists of mutual giving and taking. A couple strives to meet each other's needs. But shy singles cannot tolerate such an arrangement. Subconsciously, they demand that the opposite sex fulfill their wishes, but they are able to fulfill only a few of other persons' needs. Shy singles deal with the opposite sex on a narrow, limited basis. They greet any aggression or independence with hurt feelings or withdrawal. The partner of such an immature lover feels smothered, trapped, and restricted.

Rick, for example, was a perfect specimen of manhood. He might have been chosen to play Prince Charming in the neighborhood theater. Always courteous and polite, he treated women like china dolls. "Yes, ma'am" and "No, ma'am," he said, even to young women his own age.

His date always had to decide where they would go. Rick would not assert himself. A young woman's hopes for romance would soon turn to disappointment because she quickly realized Rick would crumble if anyone pushed against him.

What's behind this courteous marshmallow? Rick grew up viewing all women as he viewed his mother:

perfect. To hold to his viewpoint, he had to deny a lot of obvious data to the contrary. Why did Rick need to keep his mother flawless? He believed the obvious lie to avoid negative feelings about her. If his bad feelings were to surface, he feared he would no longer be worthy of his mother's love. Therefore he kept his aggression shackled. To keep himself from feeling angry, he had to see his mother as perfect.

As a child, when Rick allowed himself to express anger, his mother either ignored him or strongly disapproved. She was an intense woman who couldn't handle her own emotions well. Rick learned early: *I can't let myself be free because Mother will get mad.*

Rick has worked through many of his fears and fantasies. He realizes that he can be aggressive and still be loved. He has been willing to give up a fantasy that he is a little boy and that every female must be a mother figure. By changing his perspectives and fantasies, Rick has been able to relate to females in a more relaxed, natural fashion, allowing himself to be authentic without his former inhibitions.

Humanizing Ms. Wonder Woman

Sherry was a registered nurse—charming, educated, witty, cool, and together. As she saw her life, there was only one flaw: she was single and she wanted to be married.

"There must be something wrong with me," she concluded, "or else I'd be married." Her complaint is largely the result of the stereotype our society places on the single person. Somehow the idea comes through: To be single is to be inferior. Bank forms, loan applications, church parties, and billboards constantly remind the single person that he or she is second-class. This is changing, but the stigma is still there.

Sherry was once engaged, but she broke it off with the excuse that she wanted to fulfill her Christian commitment on a foreign field of service and her fiance did not. But what Sherry has since discovered is that she's afraid of her needs and weaknesses.

There she stands at the operating table, calmly assisting the surgeon in the middle of the patient's desperate fight for life. See her at the library checking out ponderous books on deep subjects, working at the precinct, serving coffee between church services on Sunday morning.

But probe Sherry's tender side and you touch a sensitive nerve. She stiffens and changes the subject. She displays no tenderness, no allowance for warm feelings of love. Healthy persons can be calm when their profession demands it but tender when there is a natural feeling for it. Sherry cannot handle the latter. There's the difference.

Sherry grew up in the cosmopolitan West as a middle child. Since the athletic and the charming roles had already been taken by other siblings, to find her own identity in the family she concentrated on academics. A straight-A student, she remained always rational, objectively involved in school activities but rarely able to show her tender feelings. Her parents didn't recognize the missing part of her personality. They praised her for her grades. This told Sherry she could gain praise (if not love) through intellectual pursuits.

On the surface Sherry was calm and reasonable. But on a deeper level, unknown to her, was frustration, confusion, and anger. She could not understand her dilemma until she was 35. Now she recognizes the pattern of her life. She is working through her problems, acknowledging that indeed she has tender feelings and needs to be loved and cuddled. She is allowing herself to enjoy the companionship and embraces of a man she loves, realizing that being a total person includes being tender and that acknowledging one's needs is not weakness.

Once Sherry was angry at God and her parents, but now she recognizes that Ecclesiastes 3 is correct: there is a proper time for everything. She is trying to forget the years of deprivation that she unknowingly brought on herself, and she knows that her relationships will become increasingly beautiful as she allows her total person to be expressed.

From loser to chooser

Fury is the four-letter word that is usually married to shyness. Rick knew it; Sherry embraced it; so did Howard. His experience is a clear illustration of the power one can give to the opposite sex.

Deep down Howard felt that the only thing he needed was a wife. This made females so important to him that shortly after an initial contact Howard would attempt to overwhelm and envelop them. They felt smothered and would soon break up the relationship.

After one such breakup, Howard became suicidal with rage and hopelessness. "How could she do this to me?" he repeated constantly. "The whole world is fickle. I hate it."

Howard was abandoned by his mother while he was an infant. He was raised in a variety of foster homes. And this was not the first time he'd been rejected by a young woman. His search for someone to love him had led to several crash landings. The young women who penned the "Dear John" letters did not abandon Howard because he was worthless but rather because of their own personal problems. Howard always chose young women with peculiar problems of their own.

Therapy touched several tender areas in Howard's life which jolted him awake to realities. He began to see that he was not being rejected by all humanity but rather by only one young woman at a time. He was not a helpless victim tossed on stormy emotions but rather an individual who, like everyone else, takes some losses in human relationships.

Nobody can please everybody. All of us are wonderful to some, worthless to others. Rejection by some does not mean we are worthless. Howard's terrible feelings of helplessness are fading and he is now able to say, "Hey, I am not dependent on one girl or one human relationship. If one person rejects me there are ten others who will accept me. I need to evaluate my selection procedures. I seem to be making the wrong choices."

A teacher makes the grade

No one would have suspected that sweet Sandy McClain, a painfully shy teacher of 24 years, was keeping a rather heavy dose of hatred in check. On those occasions when she permitted herself to talk with people, her mind kept wandering.

"Pardon me," she would say, much too often for her liking. "I don't understand. . . ."

In groups she was content to take no active part. She suspected that her friends had her pegged as dull and uninteresting. And she agreed with them.

In childhood, Sandy learned that among her sisters she was accepted if she kept quiet. Adventures in conversation always put her sisters on the gallop. They would outtalk her every time. Her father remained aloof, distant. Sandy established good relations with him by avoiding any expression of feeling.

Sandy contained her rage by saying nothing. She had learned: to be accepted in groups, say nothing; to avoid alienating anyone, say nothing; to maintain sweetness and light, be safe—say nothing.

Sandy's facade was shattered one day in a faculty meeting. The vote on a controversial issue was close.

The group was quite evenly divided. Finally the vote was called for. Panic gripped Sandy. The fear of separating herself from either group was so great she could not raise her hand to vote. The issue at stake seemed far less important than maintaining relationships with other people.

That's why in simple conversations Sandy would concentrate on what she was going to say next and would not hear the other speaking. Inside she had an active imagination; outside she appeared dull.

Sandy eventually realized she was a victim, not of her environment, but of her response to it.

Come-to-realize plots in fiction are deadly boring, but in therapy sessions such awakenings are golden! Somewhere in the distant past shy people elected to respond with passivity to the circumstances of their early lives. Just as they made a choice to be passive, they can make a new choice to be active. The difference is joy in place of rage and fulfillment instead of wasted years.

The pathology of perfectionism

Bashful David, a college student in his mid-20s, is afraid of females. He finds women extremely threatening. He's convinced they're out to damage his body.

Outwardly, David is composed. His hair is well-styled and he dresses impeccably. He is precise in his choice of colors and fabrics—everything he wears is "perfect."

His professors have him pegged as the ideal student, yet his counselor knows he is quite disturbed. He is headed for the ministry, where he is certain to prepare sermons reflecting his warped and twisted view of the opposite sex. His counselor will not be surprised if David is one day arrested as a child molester.

Institutions often have inadequate measures for screening their graduates. A seminary will not suspect when David enrolls that they are admitting to their student body a person who is psychologically sick. The truth will out in some tragedy along the way, to the hurt of individuals and to the embarrassment of the church.

Brian wasn't afraid of girls, as David was, but he was frustrated by his lack of ability to impress them. Weight lifting had given him a muscular body. His face was lean and handsome. But young women who were initially infatuated with him lost interest when they became better acquainted.

Brian's mother was strong, possessive. Brian was her only child, and he became the focus of her entire life. When Brian showed signs of independence, his mother, in a seductive way, would win him back. If he was going to be loved by his mother, he learned, he would have to quench his aggression and put aside any thoughts of independence. He could feel his mother's love only when he remained dependent, nonaggressive, and "sweet."

Brian was able to feel strong only when he became angry. Even then, his anger was a sham, without substance. During adolescent years he and his mother often fought, but Brian could not break the tie. Result: Brian became syrupy sweet and indecisive. Females pegged him as Mr. Milquetoast.

Women continue to intimidate Brian, but day by day he is learning to assert himself. One day he'll be a sensitive person with a good balance between tenderness and assertiveness.

How to pick a mate

Astute persons pick up clues to their prospective bride or groom during courtship. If you're considering marriage, study the parents of the other. To some degree a man or woman will be just like father and mother. If your prospective in-laws accept as normal things you heartily dislike, that should be a flashing red stop sign. Remember: you marry the family, whether you like it or not.

For another important clue, listen to the advice of friends.

A young man in seminary was kept in constant turmoil by his exasperating fiancee. His pals advised him, "Don't marry that girl. She's bad news!"

The collegian ignored their advice. He married the young woman and took her to his first pastorate. "She'll improve," he kept telling himself.

She didn't, at least not according to his liking. In a few years they were divorced. He left the ministry, disillusioned and angry at God.

It could have happened with another woman. The young pastor would not deal with his underlying personality trait that led him to marry that type of woman, so he would probably have chosen someone similar and still have ended up with a divided home.

Jane faced too late her uninspired choice. By the time she realized that her overly shy husband was not going to change his basic behavior, they had passed the point where reconciliation seemed possible. "He's not the man I married," she complained, "but come to think of it, I don't think I ever really loved him. When I married him I really thought he would overcome his shyness and provide the leadership and social life I wanted."

She didn't realize that she had fallen in love with what she wanted her husband to be, not what he really was. Ultimately their frustrations increased and their marriage dissolved. The counselor terminated the therapy sessions with the thought ringing in his head, "Why did those two ever marry each other?"

It is unfortunate but true that in this age of enlightenment and scientific endeavor, with a vast amount of information on mate selection available, young people seem to be choosing mates on a flimsier basis than ever. Certainly if the other person is not sexually attractive, admirable, and companionable, marriage should not be considered. But much more than romance and sexual attraction is needed as a basis for marriage.

Young people should ask themselves, "Can I live for 50 years with this person if they never change, if they remain exactly as they are?" If the answer is no or a hesitant yes, great caution is in order.

For the unmarried we suggest that mate selection be based on reason as well as passion. For the married we suggest that maturing as individuals will naturally bring about maturity in marriage.

Summary

Shyness in the presence of the opposite sex can be frustrating and can lead to severe loneliness. Each shy person is unique and yet common threads blend through the dynamics of shy personalities. Shyness (passivity) may be caused by a fear of intimacy. Intimacy brings about feelings of need, which in turn bring out feelings of weakness. Some persons cannot allow the weak, needy part of their personality to show. Other shy persons place members of the opposite sex on a pedestal and try to relate to these deified objects as if they themselves were unworthy serfs. This usually stems from an idealized mother or father figure.

Some singles are shy because of fear of their own aggression. They have learned in the past that their aggressiveness leads to broken relationships. Even though the relationship of parent-child is frustrating and immature, it is in these persons' eyes better than no relationship at all. Hence they remain passive, playing the role of quiescent child.

Suggestions for singles

1. Interact with people of both sexes, even though it is difficult. Begin with small, nonintimate interactions—social events (other than dating), parties at work or at school. Avoid intimate situations, but do interact with people, at least for a short time. Later, as you become more and more realistic, you will be able to tolerate greater intimacy for longer periods.

2. Study your responses to the analysis at the beginning of this book. Review them objectively and answer the following questions:

- How does the person who wrote these responses view the opposite sex?
- How does the person who wrote these responses view himself or herself?
- In view of these responses, estimate what this person had to do to gain approval from mother and father.

3. Sit down with those who know you well and ask them to describe you. Get a healthy, realistic view of yourself. Do this many times.

4. Be active in groups such as Toastmaster's Club and churches where you will, in a formal, businesslike way, interact with people. The more active you are forced to be with your environment, the sooner you will drop the passivity which has been so painful for you.

6 | IF YOU'RE MARRIED AND SHY

It is not marriage that fails, it is people that fail. All that marriage does is show people up.

HARRY EMERSON FOSDICK

Marriage is a painting, not a photograph.

Watch a master artist stroke his brush on a blank canvas. His first splash of color is bright orange down the middle, appearing to ruin the entire production. His next stroke is a blob of green in the extreme righthand corner. Surely he must be practicing! This is the warm-up period. His next stroke is a black, oval figure in the middle. As the painting emerges under the stroke of his skillful hand, the landscape begins to take shape. The orange slash becomes a stately tree, the green blob develops into hills in the background, and the dark oval is finally a blue pond which is the focus of attention.

The scene is breathtakingly beautiful. But the

beauty was missing in the early stages of filling the blank canvas.

Marriage is like that. Many young people wrongly view marriage as a photograph instead of a painting. They conceive of the wedding ceremony as the finalization of their growing up, rather than the continuation. "For better or for worse" says to them, "I hope we're compatible." They see marriage as two pieces of a jigsaw puzzle. They either fit or they don't.

Compatibility and incompatibility are myths. Marriage is not a puzzle in which each rigid piece fits or doesn't fit. Rather, marriage is a chess board—always changing, resisting closure, conformity, and snug compartmentalization. Partners who are compatible are merely those who have agreed to grow as individuals. Partners who are incompatible are those who refuse to grow. They tacitly or openly espouse the position: "I'm not going to change. If you are unhappy, then either you change or leave."

To become more compatible, one of the marriage partners will sometimes try to become what the other wants. Sooner or later the one who has attempted to conform will be torn apart by bitterness and loss of self-respect. The marriage will dissolve, first psychologically, then legally.

Relationships vary from situation to situation. Relationships during sex are different from relationships while eating dinner. Relationships while arguing are different from relationships while discussing the future. Relationships while fighting are different from relationships while shopping.

Married persons are not always aware that their relationships are constantly changing. They expect the honeymoon condition to remain throughout their married life. However, husbands and wives are extremely complex individuals. Disagreement is as much a part of marriage as is sex. Developing one's own creative potential is as much a part of marriage as is mutual love and respect. Anger is as much a part of marriage as is admiration. Marriage is a painting which is never completed, whose content is never fixed, and whose oil is never dry.

Part of being human is changing one's personality. Some changes are radical. Personalities are not fixed by the marriage ceremony. Many people experience the greatest changes of their lives after their 30s. As we grow, we change our perspectives of ourselves and other people. The relationship a couple has the day they're married cannot possibly be maintained.

A couple reared in the northwest discovered this almost too late. Ephraim was a philosophy major. He spent hours reading philosophers from Socrates to Sartre. The world of ideas fascinated him. He had little tolerance for people with a more practical mind. He was dating Julia, who showed appreciation for his philosophical ideas and admired his intellect and his facile use of six-syllable words. Part of their dating gratification centered on idealizing his intellect. He enjoyed an adoring listener.

They married, this devoted philosopher and his adoring disciple. One can't make a living nowadays reciting philosophy, so Ephraim had to acquire a teaching position, which involved relationships with people. Not everybody was as enthusiastic about his philosophy as was his wife. And even she occasionally yearned to discuss the mundane.

Marriage is a struggle not alone with words. Marriage involves flesh against flesh, will against will. Ephraim was less adept in these struggles than in the world of ideas.

Frustration and confusion mounted in him, both at home and at school. Life was no longer as exciting as it had been during the pre-marriage period. Ephraim strove harder and harder to make his philosophy work for him. And Julia poured her energies and attention into the children, the house, and activities with female companions.

There was no strife, no conflict, no close intimacy and companionship. Ephraim's obsession with words failed to get him the love he longed for but which he denied his wife. Each of them felt in some vague way that the other wasn't the person they married. The spark was gone, the honeymoon was over. Their fantasies of eternal bliss were crushed. And a kind of hopelessness prevailed.

Ephraim's strong defenses at last failed. He was overwhelmed by his fear of weakness and shattered dreams. When he realized that he needed tenderness, love, and intimacy as well as intellectual stimulation and admiration, his world turned right side up. Julia, who had been waiting for years for this to happen, accepted his weakness. Willingly she gave up her idealization of him. She began to love him in a complete, natural manner. Much to Ephraim's surprise, Julia loved him more, not less, as he admitted his fears and the way he had manipulated others into worshiping him for his facile use of words.

He changed, she changed. Each was far from the person they married. They had been eroded by frustration and aggravation. Julia took a more realistic view of herself, her husband, her neighbors, and her friends. This helped her in rearing the children. Ephraim saw that he had both strong and weak components of his personality, and he accepted his full humanity.

Their marriage now is more beautiful, more ideal than it once was. The two fully functioning human beings now pursue separate interests as well as mutual goals. They've grown, and they're happier.

Love is the final product

The term "love" has many meanings in English, ranging from a deep, intimate admiration to a quick affair between strangers. It seems almost unwise to use this word, because it means so many different things to so many different people. However, we have not found an adequate substitute.

What is love? Love is having the profound desire for the other person's maximum development and gratification. In marriage, love is doing as much as possible for the pleasure of the other person. To do the most loving thing takes a good deal of reasoning, judgment, and prayer.

In many situations we cannot know what is best for the other person. We want to protect our spouses from pain, yet we also know that sometimes pain is a necessary aspect of growing. We can sometimes show loving behavior by not interfering with the other person's pain.

Loving is not possessing. Loving is freeing the other person to be whomever he or she will be at the moment. Love is a commitment. Love is being willing to live up to the marriage vows. Love will remain through better or worse, 'til death parts. Love is committed to helping the other person to experience as much satisfaction in life as is possible.

The opposite of love is not hate, but narcissism. Narcissism is the kind of self-love that is dedicated to doing what is best for one's self. Narcissistic behavior is trying to change a spouse so he or she is more satisfactory for self. Narcissism is wanting your spouse to pay attention to you so you will feel loved. Narcissism is wanting the children to be perfectly quiet so that your world is exactly the way you want it. Narcissism is thinking that marriage would be good if your spouse would only change.

Young children are extremely narcissistic. They

have, until the age of five or six, not developed the capacity to value other people for their own right. Young children tend to appreciate parents only for what parents do for them. Very few children appreciate parents' need to go about their own business. Children feel that takes away time from them. When they want to be fed, they want to be fed *now*, regardless of what important activity the parent is involved in.

One way to describe maturity is the overcoming of normal, infantile narcissism.

If I cannot love somebody, the problem is not the other person, but my own narcissism. That statement is harsh but true. If I do not love my spouse, the problem is mine, not my spouse's. Your spouse may have many obnoxious habits and a quick temper— not at all what he or she was like before marriage. It is safe to say that no spouse is perfect. All are characterized by selfishness and many other defects. Nevertheless, if you cannot love imperfect people, the problem is yours, not theirs.

Typically, when married persons go to a counselor, they go with the idea that if the other person will change the marriage will be OK. As long as they maintain this attitude, no growth takes place and no therapy is possible. Psychologists, psychiatrists, and marriage counselors simply terminate many counseling sessions because the persons are unable to release the fantasy that their problems belong to other people. Until the individual has a strong desire to grow, little change takes place and the marriage improves little.

Grace—the basis for love

The best way to bring about growth in a spouse is to accept them exactly as they are.

Many people have the distorted notion that if they remind the other person of his weaknesses and bring these to his attention, the other person will desire to change and will take steps immediately to do so. Indeed, the opposite is true.

Persons who feel totally loved also feel secure. They understand that if they are unconditionally loved now, they will be unconditionally loved if they change. Persons who are loved change. Persons who are rejected fixate. They resist growth and change in order to maintain whatever relationships exist and to avoid further worsening of relationships. Children and spouses who feel unloved and unaccepted would rather maintain the bad relationship than risk having no relationship at all.

Remember, if you cannot accept something about your spouse, the problem lies within you. If your spouse is shy and this bothers you, ask yourself, "Why does it bother me?" If you are shy and your spouse is extroverted and you find his or her excessive social activity bothersome and threatening, ask yourself why.

Make a list of all the things about your spouse that bother you. In a column beside this list jot down how you would want your spouse to behave. Note what your ideal would be. For each of these items ask yourself, "Why do I want my spouse to behave in this 'ideal' way. What would I gain from seeing him or her act in this way? What narcissistic value is there to me to have my spouse behave this way? Why do I need to reject this part of the other person, even though I am far from perfect myself?"

Once you take the perspective that unacceptable behavior on the part of your spouse is your problem, not the other's, go to them and discuss this—with the purpose of accepting them, not changing them. The gratification you get from your spouse will be greater. And your spouse is more likely to grow and improve in that area of weakness.

How shyness affects spouses

Shyness takes many forms in marriage. Activity designed to avoid talking with one's mate indicates a shyness problem. Shyness is often a motive behind excessive reading, excessive television watching, time-consuming hobbies, extra jobs which keep one away from home, doing chores around the house when the spouse is there, and excessive talking about virtually nothing. If husband and wife are not communicating effectively and regularly, then shyness is a problem worth the attempt to alleviate.

Shyness in the sexual relationship is a problem in many thousands of marriages in which one or the other partner is afraid to actively seek gratification of his or her sexual needs, desires, and drives. For millions of married persons, sex is boring, frustrating, painful, or embarrassing. What they would really like from their partner they are too shy to ask for or to discuss. One's response to sexual situations is a barometer that accurately reveals the quality of other aspects of a relationship. There is no such thing as a merely sexual problem. Instead there are personality problems that show up in a sexual context. Let's discuss sex as an isolated topic, even though it is only a part of the total person.

What is sex about? In human beings, sex is extremely complex. Certainly it is a biological drive, but it is much more. It is a fulfillment of fantasies and wishes . . . closeness . . . lust . . . aggression . . . antagonism . . . intimacy . . . passion . . . regression to an infantile state of helplessness . . . a way of possessing the other person . . . recreation . . . an expression of love . . . the method of propagating the human species . . . the means to producing children who will be extensions of ourselves and sources of gratification. At various times sex might be all of these and none of these. It varies from time to time and place to place and age to age.

Sex at its best

The sexual experience is as varied as any aspect of personality and each experience is different from any other. We will discuss sex at its best and highest level, realizing that it will not reach these peaks on every occasion.

Ideally, sex is an extremely pleasurable experience for both partners. It is an orgy of pleasure in which each person is perfectly free to indulge their wishes and fantasies to the limit which the other person allows. Whatever loving marriage partners desire to do in their union is sanctified as long as it does not hurt either one physically or emotionally. When this freedom is established, let there be complete spontaneity.

The enemy of our souls wants every Christian marriage shattered. And if he can sow discord in the bedroom, his work is half done.

You are one with your spouse. Can any fellowship on earth be sweeter?

Preparation for the time of sex together can go on for one or two days. The anticipation of the erotic feelings adds to the pleasure of the event itself. When the husband and the wife can fantasize in anticipation of what might happen, the pleasure is extended over many hours. Satisfying sex takes good preparation.

Each couple is different. Some prepare themselves with leisurely baths; some apply fragrances that please their partners. The bedroom should be fresh, clean, and uncluttered. Preparation adds to the fun and pleasure. Keep telling the other what you'd really enjoy. Couples with healthy attitudes toward sex typically involve themselves in a variety of fore-play.

Couples who enjoy sexual experience even into their 60s, 70s, and 80s are those who have sought for a great variety of stimulation and pleasure. They are free to discover new methods of gratification. Couples that are restricted and have been inhibited by five-minute quickies soon find sex uninteresting.

Good sexual experience between husbands and wives will last from 30 minutes to two or three hours. The art of lovemaking is one of the most valuable products of human endeavor. The Old Testament reports activities including poetry, dancing, milk baths, flattery, erotic stories, feasts, and entertainment as part of the lovemaking in foreplay.

To the creative, loving, uninhibited couple, the sexual experience is the highlight of their lives and is eagerly anticipated. For a couple who are relatively mature, it is at the point of climax of the male and female (most often separated in time) where they feel the most loved, the most intimate, and the most fully united.

This is the ideal. The realities of busy married life and most sexual experiences fall far short of this. To the sexually shy, these experiences appear to be merely imaginations of the poets or the song writers and far removed from reality. For the sexually shy female, sexual intercourse can be boring and painful. She is afraid of the male aggressiveness, fearful of her lack of ability to control his passion, worried about her ability to control her own passion. She cannot relax physically or mentally, and the pain of the restricted vaginal opening is sometimes excruciating. These women often report that they can take or leave sex. They do it merely as a physical outlet for their husbands. Their husbands, sensing the wives' inhibitions, feel unloved and unmasculine, and they put intercourse on about the same level as masturbation. Many couples go through years of dull sexual experience without perceiving the possibility of improvement.

The sexually shy husband is equally a great problem. Some wives report in the clinic that they almost have to rape their husbands to get any attention at all. These husbands are so afraid of their own aggression, so afraid to leave the warm position of the presexual child-mother relationship that they are afraid to enter the "adolescent" period of sexual aggressiveness, exhibitionism, and competition. Hence they remain essentially impotent, apparently sexless persons. They can function for years as such.

One husband lived with his shy wife for seven years without once seeing any expression of sexual desire. She was afraid to be aggressive, especially in sexual union. Consequently, the husband fell prey to a seductive woman who talked him into a motel rendezvous. The thrill of being wanted sexually was so great that he willingly responded to the open enticement. He later felt compelled to admit his adultery to his wife, further driving a wedge between the antagonized female and the conscious-smitten male.

This wife, both passive-aggressive and shy-dependent, grew up on a mission field where parents taught that the female's enjoyment of sex was wrong. In truth, males enjoy their spouse's passion and sexual aggression as much as females do. People who are too shy to express sexual interest will have spouses who are not fully gratified.

Sexual shyness is a major problem. Procedures that will help a person overcome shyness in general will help to overcome shyness during sexual periods. Any couple not getting full gratification out of their sexual experience is hurting. The attitude, "I can take it or leave it," is a sham. If you leave it, you and your partner are frustrated.

Promiscuity as shyness

Going to bed with a variety of sexual partners is a form of shyness. The promiscuous are deeply afraid of knowing and being known. They deliberately separate love and sexuality in their representation of themselves and in their behavior because they are afraid of love.

Very often promiscuous persons have a great deal of hatred toward the opposite sex. They use sex to get revenge for some deep-seated wrong which occurred in childhood. Promiscuous females seek sexual involvement to get the male into positions of weakness, need, and helplessness, thereby fulfilling their wishes to be strong. Promiscuous males often fear the power that females have over them. So rather than enter into competition with females in terms of intelligence, they use sex and physical strength to overcome vulnerable women, thus enhancing their feeling of power. This is a reenactment of childhood fantasies and a fear of moving into and through sexual adolescence.

Divorced and shy

Separated mates cannot avoid the relentless question: How much is the divorce my responsibility and how much is it my former mate's? Many tend to put major responsibility on the other person to avoid the feeling of personal failure. In most cases it is impossible to pinpoint the causes of divorce. Marriages are complicated. Each partner brings a total personality into marriage situations with his or her own wishes, expectations, and fears. Finding the exact cause of separation is usually useless and impossible. It is better to encourage divorced people to orient their lives toward present realities and growth rather than to the past.

Hope for failing marriages

Nearly all divorces can be prevented. For persons who are divorced, planning divorce, or headed for divorce, there is hope of improved relationships. If shyness is a factor in the poor relationships, overcoming it will be helpful.

Most often only one partner is really open to change during periods of conflict between mates. When one person changes and mellows in his rigid attitudes, the other person is soon likely to be open to change as well.

One of the mates must begin to change. One needs to be brave enough to say, "I know my mate is not perfect, but I can't change that. I will go about making myself the best person possible. And if that brings about improvement in the marriage, so much the better."

The goal of any improvement in marriage is for one or both of the partners to improve as persons.

The excitement of openness

Simple answers are no solution to problems developing from shyness. However, if a couple will be fully open with each other, their marriage will be greatly strengthened. As we become more and more open and expand our ability to verbalize our feelings, we discover more about ourselves.

There are always new things to be open about. The inner landscape of human personalities is so vast and complex, so varied and exciting, it would take much more than a lifetime to fully explore. Persons who are open about themselves in their 20s will find other things to be open about in their 30s, 40s, 50s, and 60s. Persons who have been married to each other for 40 or 50 years report new discoveries about their mates and about themselves.

Both spouses must be open to discussions. Persons who say, "I'd like to talk about myself but there's nothing to say," are really saying, "I don't want to talk about myself." There is no such thing as having nothing to say about one's self.

Tell your mate something new about yourself that you have not yet communicated. Couples who start down the road of openness are surprised at how willing their partners are to hear weaknesses and fears and strange ideas verbalized by the other. As a married partner moves toward greater freedom, the other typically feels more and more free. Slowly they both begin to see themselves as total human beings.

Summary

Sexual shyness in marriage is a problem for millions of persons. It is a problem that can be solved. Sex is a part of the total personality and any time the total personality grows, the sexual relationship improves.

7 | WHEN SHYNESS IS AN ASSET

*If you're shy,
you're in good company.*

THE AUTHORS

Each aspect of an individual's personality can be both a liability and an asset. Shyness is no exception.

Shyness, like boldness, good looks, ugliness, strength, weakness, is neither good nor bad per se. Most often these traits have both positive and negative values.

Most people would prefer to be good-looking rather than ugly, but even good looks can be a liability. A well-known movie star once wrote an article titled, "It's Hell to Be Handsome." He related the difficulties good-looking people have in being treated as equals. For this man, his good looks produced many unpleasant experiences. They contributed, he felt, to his loneliness.

A girl who grew up in the bayou country of Louisiana spoke with a tick in her speech—a slight clicking sound on certain consonants. To compensate, she developed a beautiful singing voice and a moving, dramatic manner of delivery. In her singing there was no impediment.

Her self-concept as a singer was:

I am prepared
I know what I'm going to sing
I can concentrate on making others feel good
I can be of value

Her self-concept in conversation was:

I have this tick
I might be laughed at
Therefore, I must watch carefully what I say
So I can't pay attention to other people's needs

A 30-year-old male, single and extremely shy, found he could excel as an athlete. "It's the only way I can relate to other males," Russ admitted. "I quit two jobs because they interfered with basketball."

For this lean and lanky cager, it was a good idea to drop out of work. He needed communication with people more than he needed his salary. In the structured environment of basketball, where the topic was understood, Russ felt free. The pounding of that ball drew out his aggression in a legitimate way. The better he became at basketball, the better he felt about himself.

England's illustrious Prime Minister Winston

Churchill became a famous orator largely because of shyness. Since he was ineffective and weak in conversation, he worked hard to develop a commanding oratory. His speeches roused a nation to fight during World War II. His messages to youth are still remembered. One evening as the prime minister stood before a class of young men graduating from an elite academy, his entire speech consisted of six eloquent words: "Never give up. Never . . . never . . . never!" His parliamentary oratory is recorded in large volumes.

Typical of Sir Winston's abbreviated but beautiful style was this postwar tribute to England's young men who flew in the Royal Air Force during World War II: "Seldom have so many owed so much to so few."

His contemporary in the United States, President Franklin D. Roosevelt, was poor in one-to-one communication. This forced him to develop as a public speaker, and his eloquence stimulated a discouraged nation struggling out of the Great Depression.

Two-cycle feedback

The vicious cycle of shyness is well known. Shy individuals approach a social situation with fear of doing or saying the wrong thing. Because of this, they lack confidence, are not assertive, and pay too much attention to their behavior and words.

Because of these factors, their prophecies of social inadequacies come true. They don't sound confident, therefore people don't value their statements. Since they are trying so hard to please, they burst into conversations with poor timing and irrelevant topics. Because of their attention to themselves and their relationships with others, they do not give full attention to what the others are saying and to the exterior world. People are uncomfortable with shy persons' introspection and intensity.

As a result of this self-fulfilling prophecy, shy persons become more reluctant to talk. They walk away from distressful social situations with the attitude, "That proves that I'm not worthwhile because I can't influence people and get them to pay attention to me." Through this cycle the shy syndrome is strengthened and maintained.

But there is also a growth cycle that has been beneficial to many shy persons. Many reached greatness as a compensation for their shyness. Shy persons who fear free conversation may gain an identity and a reputation through athletics, artistry, or public speaking.

As they become active in such areas, shy persons begin to get a different, more positive perspective of themselves. Positive feedback from other persons reinforces their feelings of worth. They ride the coattails of individual strength to a much-improved self-image and feel less need to gain attention through conversation.

As shy persons become interested in something outside themselves, they become much more interesting to talk to. Other people pay attention to what they say. They complete a growth cycle through their efforts to compensate for shyness.

The bright side

Characteristics of shyness are not all bad. Shy people lend grace to our society. They do not want to offend. Such shyness is a necessary part of healthy interpersonal relationships. Factors that contribute to shyness also contribute to caring about how we appear to others and to ourselves. Without this concern our society would be chaotic. We adopt acceptable standards of behavior so that we do not alienate people. We develop certain rituals, such as saying "Hello" or "How are you?" or "Have a good day," to relate to people when there is no time for intimacy.

The degree and kind of shyness we experience may greatly influence our choice of vocation. Careers that draw unusually large numbers of applications from among the shy include accounting, computer programming, engineering, laboratory technicians, acting, and research science. These are all careers in which direct, unstructured communication with other people is minimal. Persons who are less shy and who find conversation gratifying may not be able to tolerate the long periods of isolation that these and similar jobs demand.

Shyness is an advantage in a variety of vocations, including the following:

Counseling　　Shy people are often excellent listeners. Because of their passivity, they don't interrupt or rush to give their own opinions when others talk. Because they are sensitive about their own feelings, they are sensitive about the feelings of others and they are intuitive. A counselor who sits in an office listening to other people all day long has to enjoy that role. The socially active persons may not be able to tolerate so much passivity, but shy people are comfortable listening to others.

The very shy may also be passive in their counseling. Persons who are less shy are more apt to be active in giving advice.

Art Most artists, be their discipline drama, oils, music, or sculpting, are more satisfied and at ease working with their medium than they are conversing with people. For them conversation is limiting. They find greater creative expression in their media, which allow them to go beyond the mere connotations of talking. Many persons are much more able to communicate in writing, in poetry, or in painting than they are in face-to-face verbalization. Those who get their gratification through verbalization do not feel the intense need to express themselves in the other media and are less likely to be creative, quality artists.

Public speaking Talented public speakers are often shy. To overcome their shyness they prepare exceedingly well their speeches and talks. Persons for whom verbal communication comes easy are not likely to feel the need to perfect their speeches to such a high degree and will not spend the time necessary to develop outstanding messages.

Politicians, ministers, promoters, and, to a certain degree, salesmen, often are motivated to excel in oratory because of basic shyness.

One of the most influential speakers on the West Coast in the early twentieth century was, according to his own words, "terrified" in informal groups. But he was purely elated when he was speaking in front of a large audience.

Writing The discipline of writing requires long, sometimes tedious periods in private, grooming a manuscript for a publisher. Not many gregarious people could tolerate long stretches of time in a writer's cubicle drafting stories, articles, essays, or poetry. Shy people are unusually well adapted to the discipline of writing.

Teaching Many teachers of young people feel shy around adults. They get their gratification through leading young people into greater heights of thinking and creative behavior.

While in college, Bertha was obese, homely, withdrawn, and largely ignored by her peers. She went through the entire four and a half years necessary to get her teaching credentials without any notable accomplishment. Her professors had to look in the college annual to be reminded of who she was so they could write letters of recommendation. Prospects for success in teaching seemed minimal.

Her first assignment was a second-grade class in a

Los Angeles suburban school. Almost immediately in front of her class of seven-year-olds she blossomed into a marvelous leader and inspiring teacher. Within three years she was asked to become a consultant for her district, helping other teachers develop their skills. She became known as one of the outstanding teachers in southern California. Other districts called her in for consultation. She worked at her appearance and became a thoroughly attractive, highly successful teacher.

The shy laugh last

Persons most to be pitied in our society are not the shy but rather the glib who have learned in childhood to charm their way through life with wit and nerve. They've learned to overcome frustration by talking their way out of it. They enjoy positive feedback from people without excelling in their endeavors. They talk instead of learn; they become shallow.

In the long run, the shy person has a more realistic view of the world than the person for whom conversation is a breeze, for whom attention is never lacking, to whom compliments are always generous. Conversation can serve as a stimulant, making the talker feel good all over without the depression and therefore without the growth required of the shy.

Shy people have accomplished marvelous things. If you're shy, you're in good company!

8 | THE SHYNESS CLINIC

Each mind has its own method.
EMERSON

"Can I overcome my shyness?"

"Will I be able to live relatively free from that excruciating anxiety which I experience in social situations?"

"Is it possible that I can eventually relate to people freely, without having to weigh every word . . . suffer fear each time I express an idea?"

The answer to each question above is yes. Shyness can be alleviated. People of any age who are motivated to overcome their social handicap can make great progress by following the program outlined in this chapter.

There is no rapid, simple solution to the problem of shyness. The length of time required to overcome the problem differs from person to person. The program might last from one to five years, but some help should be arranged immediately. By following the steps given below, most persons should greatly enhance their social confidence and skill.

Step 1: Commence

By reading this book, you have already begun your therapy. Do not expect your shyness, which has probably developed over many years, to be overcome immediately. If you had started therapy five years ago, you would not be suffering as you are today. If you start now, in five years you will be radically different.

Step 2: Diagnose

The second step is to determine the general causes of your shyness. You may not understand completely the full ramifications, but it is important that you start the investigation.

Determine roughly which category of shyness you are in. If you are in the shy-terrified category, by all means seek long-range professional help. If you are shy-anxious, professional help will improve your chances for more rapid and more complete amelioration of your problem.

Step 3: Verbalize

Find someone who will listen to you as you explore the complex caverns of your mind. Consider yourself and that other person to be a spelunker—

you're exploring hitherto unexamined caves and grottoes of the mind, and you have no idea what you will find. It will be a very exciting, profitable exploration.

Choose someone who will not give advice, who does not feel the need to mother you. The person should have a deep appreciation of who you are at the moment and great confidence in people's ability to grow. Pick someone who is strong enough so that you will not be able to manipulate them into being active or who in other ways is unable to handle your passive tendencies.

Do not choose a spouse or a business associate. It is almost impossible for such persons to be helpful to you because of their own personal investment in the relationship. They will unconsciously want you to remain the same as you are for their sakes.

It is important that the person you choose understands that they are not to give advice. Make sure they do not fill in for you when you desire to remain silent, or feel pity for you because of your dilemma.

Step 4: Probe

Talk . . . talk . . . talk . . . talk . . . talk. . . . Once your listener has agreed to the program, start divulging and expressing your feelings and opinions on any and all subjects that your mind brings up, no matter how trivial or boring.

The important thing is for you to say everything and anything that you think of during your counseling sessions. Concentrate on expressing your feelings at the moment. Don't say much about other times and other places. What is happening outside your counseling sessions is not as important at this stage. Do or be whatever you want to do or be.

You will be tempted to make excuses, to complain that you have nothing to say, to label the whole program "ridiculous, a waste of time." You might object that it's unnatural for the other person to be so quiet and decide that you might as well quit now because, obviously, this program is not working.

All of these will be your attempts to ward off the fear that arises as you leave your secure, passive position. Most people quit at this step. If you can hurdle the temptation to quit, growth will begin to be visible and steady. This stage might last weeks or months.

Step 5: Be aware

At this stage, make an effort to gain insights about yourself. Most people believe they are aware of their motives and the dynamics of how they relate to people, but actually most people's insight is minimal. Some shy-anxious types have strong feelings which give them a sense of awareness, but their insight is superficial and inaccurate. You will begin to find out that you have intentionally, although unconsciously, distorted your view of yourself and other people.

As you talk, ask yourself, "What am I feeling toward my listener?" At first you may feel very little. Then you are likely to begin to be aware that you are angry toward the other person. You will want to deny your anger, because anger will not fit in with your wish to be perfect.

Monitor these insights carefully. What are you really feeling in your counseling sessions and in other social situations? All of our wishes reveal what we really expect of ourselves and others. Ultimately shy people are afraid to let themselves *feel*. They're afraid of what they'll *do* if they let themselves go. They're afraid they might make a hostile comment or attack some person or hug and embrace someone. As you are talking, ask yourself, "What am I expecting of myself? What do I want the other person to do?"

Some people are helped most when asked to produce images of themselves and the other person listening. Watch these images and see what unfolds. This will give you insight into what you really want from the other person. If the other person appears angry, then you are angry. If the other person is kind, you seek tenderness. If the other person appears aloof, you are afraid to give warm, loving feelings to this other person. Whatever feelings you attribute to the other person in these mental images are probably your own feelings.

You will try repeatedly to give the ball back to the counselor, to ask for his or her insights and explanations. But it will be better if, for the most part, you gain your own insights. The process of developing your own understanding is more important at this stage than being accurate.

Step 6: Develop insights

At first you may make excuses in order to withdraw from your therapy. You will criticize the program. You will catch a glimpse of how you have tried to control people in order to maintain your own passivity. You will recognize your own anger, your fear of criticism, and your striving for perfection in yourself and others.

You will see how you have schemed to get other people to do and say things for you. You will realize that your conversations have been superficial, that you have not taken each bit of conversation for its own value and given it your full attention. You will begin to realize that in all social situations you have been hoping to impress rather than to understand the other person. You haven't cared about other people and their ideas. Now with the facts before you, there is opportunity for sensible change and beneficial recovery.

By the time you reach this stage you will begin to realize that social situations are somehow easier, less tense, and more relaxing for you. Your dependency on the counselor will diminish. You will sense that you are a more complete person. You have overcome your fear of being active. You see yourself as a stronger, more realistic individual.

Learn to tolerate fluctuation of moods (particularly anger and depression). They are a necessary part of the maturing process. Do not fear them. Let them usher you through new insights to a more beautiful tomorrow.

Mario lay weeping on the couch. Tears welled from a combination of intense relief and sadness—relief that he could accept himself as imperfect, and sadness that he had burdened himself for 44 years with the struggle to be perfect in order to be loved.

"I feel a hundred pounds lighter!" he sighed.

He cried unashamedly on the couch, remembering the wasted years which had brought him resentment and sorrow. Crying is OK for a man. It's not OK for a god. But Mario was finally ready to admit that he wasn't a god and therefore could cry.

The joy and pleasure that comes from this stage of therapy is indescribable. Shy persons realize they no longer have to live up to an image. They accept themselves as they are: neither perfect nor terrible, but OK. The months, years, and decades that have passed in previous states of shyness are almost worth the waiting as people come to this marvelous discovery.

No longer a victim

As you carry out this six-step program, you will gain deep and specific insights about yourself. The main thing you will discover is that you are not a victim of your environment. As you continue to talk, you will begin to see yourself not as helpless but as active in controlling your environment.

Your social life will improve greatly. Anxiety will be reduced. Your view of the world will become more realistic. You will come to see yourself neither as monstrously bad nor perfectly good, but somewhere in between. In general you will trust people. You will develop the confidence and the sense of wholeness that come with maturity.

No longer will you desire to be the center of attention in all social situations. No longer will you be afraid to express your feelings openly. You will find yourself liking more people and loving some intimately.

Shyness will become a minor problem and you will wonder why it was so bothersome in past years. You will be free to be whatever you can be without the fetters of isolation, perfectionism, striving, and anxiety.

At this point in therapy the Christian begins to appreciate fully the doctrine of grace. "God accepts me not because of who *I* am but because of who *he* is. He loves me not because I deserve it. He loves me not from pity. He loves me because I am a human being and he is God. Nothing I can do is so awful that God will stop loving me."

Romans 8:38-39 burns through to shy Christians in its majestic truth: Nothing, nothing, nothing can separate us from the love of God. No matter how despicable we have been or might become, God loves us.

Principles to remember during therapy

1. Lasting behavioral changes occur as our vision of ourselves and the world changes. Unless we alter the way we see ourselves and others, behavioral changes will be temporary at best.

2. Healing takes time. After many years, shyness is deeply entrenched. You must alter many concepts and many feelings. Time itself does not heal. It only offers a variety of experiences to allow growth to take place.

3. Growth, for the most part, comes only through interaction with another. Shy persons who do not obtain feedback from other people do not grow. Only by talking in the presence of another and expressing feeling toward that person can we gain insights into ourselves.

4. Gaining insights, however, is only half the prescription for change. The other half is entering into a situation where passivity fails to maintain satisfactory relationships. As long as shy persons remain in situations they can control by remaining passive and getting others to be active, they won't change. Change comes only when old ways of relating to people fail. That's why it is extremely important at the start of therapy to select a listener who will not intervene to support your passivity.

5. Perspectives change with experience. Things

you say early in therapy will be different from things you say later in the relationship. If you're not changing, you're not growing. Every way you think and feel now is likely to be different to some degree as you grow. Expect alterations in your vision of the world.

6. Perfection is not the goal. Rather, the goal is to accept yourself as an imperfect human and to give up the fantasy that you are godlike in your perfection.

7. Selfishness, anger, loss of memory, failure—all these will not seem as alarming as they once did. You will come to recognize that imperfections are an essential part of human existence. We are not gods, nor will we ever be gods. Accepting our humanity is the only way to become fully human. Scripture's essential message is that we are imperfectly human and therefore need a relationship with a perfect God. God's rivals are not pagan gods, but each person's desire to be his or her own god.

9 | PERSPECTIVE

To be rather than to seem
MOTTO OF LORD SOMERS

Life is never perfect; life can always be improved. We vessels of clay must learn to cope with varied degrees of depression, anxiety, and disappointment between the refreshing rains of spiritual restoration. To expect nothing but the idyllic is unrealistic—even pathological.

The imperfections you may be suffering today are nobody's fault. Blaming our parents is futile, for then they must blame their parents until finally responsibility is lost.

In one sense you are not to be blamed either for your shyness. Your choices to be passive toward people were made long before you were capable of understanding the implications or the far-reaching consequences. You are responsible not for the past, not for the future, but for the present. What you do today is your complete responsibility. If you continue seeing yourself and your environment as you have in the past, your future will be the same as your present. You can grow only if you stop seeing yourself as better than you really are.

It's up to you

Here, for handy reference, are 13 reminders representing the main points of this book. If you apply these directives, shyness will be only a minor problem and your life will blossom into new and exciting dimensions.

Reminder 1: People of all ages experience shyness. Most hide it, but no one has escaped at least occasional anxiety.

Reminder 2: Shyness can be an asset. Shy people listen, create, reflect, plan, further science, scrub, and beautify the world. They are sensitive to social needs and are among the most helpful, nurturing people in our society.

Reminder 3: Being shy is not morally or ethically bad. Extroverted people might be more popular, but they are not more worthy. Worth depends on character—your value system and your behavior. Shyness is not related to a person's worth.

Reminder 4: Shyness results from a vast number of causes. No two shy persons are alike. Each grew up with different adults and surroundings, each responded differently to the environment, and each will solve the problem of shyness differently.

Reminder 5: Though shy people tend to consider the non-shy to be in better mental health, extroverts are often more disturbed and suffer more intensely poor self-concepts than the shy. Extreme extroversion is generally a method of avoiding an honest look within, fearing the discovery of disturbing inadequacies.

Reminder 6: Shy people are not victims of measures beyond their control. Each chooses the behavior and the world vision that seems efficient at the time. Thousands of choices from infancy to old age shape our destiny.

Reminder 7: Most bashful people feel they were intimidated by their environment and robbed by others of a chance to develop conversational skills. But shyness is not a problem primarily of verbal skill. It is more wide-ranging. It is a deliberate choice to remain passive in the presence of other people in order to maintain the fantasy of perfect relationships.

Reminder 8: Shyness is often maintained to cover up bad feelings. Most are willing to endure the anxiety and embarrassment of shyness because it masks the frightening anger and depression that lie near the surface.

Reminder 9: Shyness is a device to avoid what the timid consider to be threatening changes in how they view themselves and the world. They would rather cling to fantasies than test them by being active.

Reminder 10: Any experience that forces shy persons to fail in maintaining hypocritical human relationships fosters growth. It can cause beneficial change in their representation of themselves and the world. Maturity comes from interaction with other people. Feedback from other people is absolutely necessary for growth.

Reminder 11: Changes occur gradually. Dramatically swift changes rarely sustain themselves. Piece by piece, bit by bit, slowly . . . slowly our view of ourselves and the world becomes more realistic.

Reminder 12: Do not be afraid of who you are at the moment. You are constantly changing. Next year you will not be the same person you are today. As you move toward maturity, many transpositions will alter your perspective. Face each one fairly. Accept yourself today and you will better accept maturity tomorrow.

Pray that God will send experiences, situations, and people into your life to help you become less shy and give you a deeper appreciation for God's wisdom and love in creating you the way you are.

Pray that you will be able to drop your defense against enjoying life as God intended.

Ask God to help you approach nearer and nearer unto mature stature so you will be able to enjoy fully the world our heavenly Father created for you.

SELF-ANALYSIS EVALUATION

*Understanding your responses
to the self-analysis on pages 13-16.*

1. This is not altogether reliable, but it can indicate your general emotional status. The circle symbolizes sexual desire for both men and women. The square indicates structure, organization, and security. The star expresses anger or hostility, and the S suggests looseness, disorganization, and escape. Which did you use most? If you used only one or two symbols, you may have problems in the areas indicated above. Probably healthier people use a variety of symbols. If you find yourself avoiding any of these symbols, it also means denial of the area indicated by the symbol.

2. Is the role you selected to play the "true" you, what you wish to be? Did you select a passive, secondary role or an active, dominant one? As you thought of the various roles, how did you conceive them? What does this tell you concerning the way you conceive of yourself?

3 and 4. The "why" is the key. Did you choose an animal or person because of beauty, strength, ability

to escape, timidity, playfulness, or what? The attribute you chose is probably the opposite of how you really think you are. It more accurately represents what you *wish* you were.

5. Immaturity in your sexual autobiography will be indicated by either one of two trends.

Trend 1: Denial and anxiety. Were you completely honest about your fantasies and fears? If you felt inhibited, you have not accepted sexuality as a normal part of self. You probably have strong sexual desires but want to deny them.

Mature people are cognizant of themselves and do not need to deny anything. Sexuality should be seen as basically a good aspect of self.

Trend 2: Look for superficiality, depersonalization, and perversion in your sexual autobiography. Many persons are not able to feel warmth toward others. To them, sexuality is not seen as a way of communicating but merely as a way to gain power, revenge, or gratification. As these persons mature, sex becomes more personal and private. The so-called perversions (excessive masturbation, fetishism, voyeurism, etc.) are ways of avoiding intimacy.

6. Shyness autobiography
   a. With whom are you most shy?
   b. With whom are you least shy?
   c. How do those persons treat you?
   d. What do you do to avoid shy feelings—joke, dominate, seduce, act helpless?

e. What fantasies (daydreams) do you have?

f. What did you feel when your parents criticized you as a child and as an adolescent?

g. What did you feel when a sibling (or peer) dominated conversations with you?

h. What did you imagine yourself doing to gain attention in your family or in another group of people?

i. What did you actually do to gain attention in your family or other groups?

7. As you read your sentence completions, what do you learn? Stand back and view your answers objectively. Treat them as if someone else had answered them. Write a brief summary about "the person" who completed the sentences. Talk about the person's needs, wishes, fears, inhibitions, and grasp of reality.